MACMILLAN READERS

PRE-INTERMEDIATE LEVEL

Selected Short Stories by D. H. Lawrence

Retold by Anne Collins

MACMILLAN

MACMILLAN READERS

PRE-INTERMEDIATE LEVEL

Founding Editor: John Milne

The Macmillan Readers provide a choice of enjoyable reading material for learners of English. The series is published at six levels – Starter, Beginner, Elementary, Pre-intermediate, Intermediate and Upper.

Level Control
Information, stucture and vocabulary are controlled to suit the students' ability at each level.

The number of words at each level:

Starter	about 300 basic words
Beginner	about 600 basic words
Elementary	about 1100 basic words
Pre-intermediate	about 1400 basic words
Intermediate	about 1600 basic words
Upper	about 2200 basic words

Vocabulary
Some difficult words and phrases in this book are important for understanding the story. Some of these words are explained in the story, some are shown in the pictures, and others are marked with a number like this: ...[3]. Words with a number are explained in the Glossary at the end of the book.

Answer Keys
Answer Keys for the *Points for Understanding* and *Exercises* sections can be found at www.macmillanenglish.com

Contents

A Note About the Author and These Stories

David Herbert Lawrence was born on 11th September, 1885, in Eastwood, Nottinghamshire, a county[1] in the north of England. His father was a miner[2] and his mother had been a teacher. The Lawrences were poor and their marriage was not happy. They often quarrelled[3]. They had five children and David Herbert Lawrence was their fourth child.

D. H. Lawrence was a weak child and he was often ill, but he was also intelligent and sensitive[4]. His relationship[5] with his mother was very close. Lawrence's mother loved him very deeply and she wanted him to succeed. She did not want him to be a miner, like his father. So she made sure that he went to school. Lawrence won a scholarship[6] in 1898 and attended Nottingham High School. But when he was fifteen, he had to leave school and take a job. At this time, he met Jessie Chambers, the daughter of a farmer. In 1906, Lawrence won a scholarship to Nottingham University College and began his studies to be a teacher.

In 1911, Lawrence's mother died and his first book, *The White Peacock*, was published. In the same year, Lawrence ended his relationship with Jessie Chambers and got engaged[7] to Louie Burrows. But he also became seriously ill. He had tuberculosis, a disease of the lungs. Lawrence could not continue his career as a teacher. He began to write. He wanted to earn money by writing books and poetry.

Lawrence met Frieda Weekley in 1912. She was married to a professor who had taught Lawrence at Nottingham University. Frieda was German and six years older than Lawrence, and she had three children. Lawrence and Frieda fell deeply in love and they ran away together.

Lawrence and Frieda never had much money and their passionate[8] relationship was difficult. They often quarrelled.

But their lives together gave Lawrence many ideas for his books. He wrote travel books about the places that they visited. And he wrote short stories and novels about the relationships between lovers, parents and children, wives and husbands. His stories shocked many people.

Lawrence's health was bad so he was unable to fight in the First World War (1914–18). He spent this time in England and became friends with many famous and clever people.

Frieda got her divorce in 1914 and she married Lawrence on 13th July, 1914. By this time, Lawrence had written *The Trespasser* (1913), and his first big novel, *Sons and Lovers* (1913). His next novel, *The Rainbow* (1915), brought him trouble with the law. All copies of the book were taken by the police. People were shocked because the story talked about sex in strong, plain language.

In 1916, Lawrence finished writing his novel, *Women in Love*, but no one would publish it. At last, a publisher in New York published the book in 1920, and it was published in London in 1921. From 1922, Frieda and Lawrence travelled to many countries. They went to Sri Lanka, Australia, the United States and Mexico. While he was in Australia, Lawrence wrote *Kangaroo*, which was published in 1923. And in the same year, *Studies in Classic American Literature* was published.

Lawrence was always worried about money and his health became worse. At this time, his relationship with Frieda also became more difficult. While he was in Mexico, he began to write *The Plumed Serpent* and he also wrote many short stories and poems. In 1923, Frieda returned to Europe alone. Frieda and Lawrence wrote many letters to each other and finally, Lawrence returned to England. But he was very unhappy and early the next year, they went to live at Kiowa Ranch in New Mexico, in the United States.

In 1925, Lawrence became seriously ill. The tuberculosis was killing him. The Lawrences went to live in Italy, where Lawrence began to paint pictures. He finished writing his last novel, *Lady Chatterley's Lover,* in Florence. The book brought him the worst trouble of his career. It told the story of a rich, married woman who has a sexual relationship with a man who works for her husband. *Lady Chatterley's Lover* was published privately in Florence in 1928, by a friend of Lawrence's. But thirty years passed before the whole novel was published in the United States and Britain. Penguin Books, the publishers, had to have a trial in a court before they could print the book.

In June 1929, Frieda took Lawrence to doctors in Germany and France. But they could not make him well. He died in Vence, France, on 2nd March, 1930. He was forty-four years old.

D. H. Lawrence was one of the most important British authors of the twentieth century. He wanted all important things to be discussed freely. And he believed that people should live their lives completely. He thought that women should be free to live how they wished. He upset many people, but he also made them think about their own relationships and beliefs.

Many of Lawrence's short stories were collected together and appeared in three volumes in 1955. He wrote *Love Among the Haystacks* in 1911 and rewrote it in 1913. *The Virgin and the Gipsy* and *The Rocking Horse Winner* were both written in 1926. *The Lovely Lady* was written in 1927. His travel books are: *Twilight in Italy* (1916), *Sea and Sardinia* (1921), *Mornings in Mexico* (1927) and *Etruscan Places* (1932).

At this time, British money was *pounds* (£), *shillings* (s) and *pence* (d). There were 12 pennies (pence) in 1 shilling and 20 shillings (s) in 1 pound (£). Measurements were in *miles, yards, feet* and *inches*. 1 inch = 25.3995 mm, 1 foot = 30.479 cm, 1 yard = 0.9144 m, 1 mile = 1.6093 km.

These stories were written just after the First World War, which took place in western Europe, Poland and western Russia. More than 8 million people died, and over 16 million people were wounded in the First World War.

There were many changes in the 1900s. There were new ideas in medicine, politics, technology and fashion. People rode in cars and trains, instead of using horses and carriages. Women began to make more decisions about their lives and their money. They wanted to choose who they loved and married. They also changed the style of their clothes and their hair. Before 1910, women had worn their hair long. After this time, many women cut their hair short. And by 1929, British women were able to vote. They could choose the people who governed the country.

Films have been made of the stories, *The Virgin and the Gipsy* (1970, UK) and *The Rocking Horse Winner* (1949, UK).

THE VIRGIN AND THE GIPSY[9]

Lucille and Yvette Saywell were sisters. When Lucille was nine years old and Yvette was seven, a shocking thing happened in their family. Their mother, Cynthia, left their father and ran away with a young, poor man.

The sisters' father, Arthur Saywell, was a vicar[10]. He was a handsome man and a good husband. The vicar's neighbours[11] were very surprised. Why had the vicar's wife left him?

Lucille and Yvette did not know why their mother had gone away. Perhaps she did not love them. Perhaps they had not been good daughters.

The vicar was offered a job as rector of Papplewick, a small village in the north of England. So the family went to live in the rectory, which stood just outside the village. The rectory was an ugly stone house, with the River Papple running just beside it.

The rector's mother, and his sister Aunt Cissie, came to live with the rector and his two daughters. The rector's mother – or Granny, as the girls called her – was over seventy years old. The rector was very upset that his wife had left. So Granny never spoke about Cynthia to her son. But, secretly, the old woman was pleased that Cynthia had run away. Granny was now the most important person in the house. She controlled everybody else so that they did what she wanted. She liked controlling the family very much. If Cynthia came back, everything would change. And Granny did not want that to happen.

Lucille and Yvette remembered their first home in the south, very clearly. They also remembered their mother. She had been like the sun. She was beautiful and bright, but also dangerous. She had brought light and life to the house, but she had also been selfish.

As Granny grew older, she became almost blind. She could not read and somebody had to lead her about because she could see very little. She did not get out of her bed until midday, but she controlled all the other people in the house.

The rector especially loved his younger daughter, Yvette. Yvette was like her mother in many ways. She was beautiful but careless. The rector spoiled[12] Yvette. And he let her do everything that she wanted. So, as Yvette grew up, she did not care very much about other people's feelings.

The rector's sister, Aunt Cissie, was almost fifty. She spent all her time taking care of Granny. Cissie did not complain[13], but inside she felt angry. She had no life of her own and no future. She had no time for herself. And she had nothing to look forward to[14]. Yvette was young and beautiful. She never tried to understand Aunt Cissie's feelings. So Aunt Cissie was jealous of Yvette and hated her.

When they had finished their education in England, Lucille and Yvette were sent to a school in Switzerland for a year. They returned to the rectory at Papplewick when Lucille was twenty-one and Yvette was nineteen. They were tall, attractive young girls with fresh, bright faces. Their hair was cut short in the modern style.

It was a summer day and Yvette and Lucille were coming back to England. They were crossing the Channel by boat from France. The girls were not looking forward to living at the rectory.

'Papplewick is such a boring place,' said Yvette. 'There are no interesting young men living near the village.'

'Yes, there are!' said Lucille. 'The Framley family lives in the village and Bob Framley is a nice young man. And you know that Gerry Somercotes adores you.'

'But men who adore me are *very* boring,' said Yvette. 'I would like to fall deeply in love.'

'I wouldn't,' said Lucille. 'I would hate to fall in love.

Perhaps you would hate it too, if it happened.'

'But won't you hate to go back to Papplewick?' said Yvette.

'Not really,' said Lucille. 'But I suppose that we'll get rather bored there. I wish that Daddy would buy a car. We'll have to ride our bicycles everywhere.'

As the ship came closer to the south coast of England, Yvette and Lucille watched the cliffs of Dover. The walls of rock were usually white when the sun shone. But today, the sky was grey and dull, and the cliffs were grey and dull too.

The two girls looked tall and confident[15]. But they were just young girls who knew nothing about life. They were like ships that were moving from a safe harbour onto the wide and dangerous sea.

As soon as they went inside the rectory, Lucille and Yvette felt depressed[16] . The hard stone walls seemed ugly and unclean. The furniture seemed ugly and unclean too. Nothing was fresh. The food they ate was terrible. Granny was given special things to eat. And grey-faced Aunt Cissie ate very little – only one boiled potato at dinner. She never ate meat. Cissie hated food and eating.

Granny was now over eighty years old. It was easy for her to control her son. When Arthur Saywell's marriage went wrong, he had realized that life outside the family could be difficult and dangerous. Only life inside the family was safe. So he stayed close to the family and his mother – the most important person in the house.

The countryside[17] round the village of Papplewick was dark and dull, with steep hills and deep, narrow valleys. All the houses in the village were made of stone. Life in Papplewick was as dull as stone too.

Lucille got a job in the city as a secretary[18]. She travelled to and from the city every day, by train. Both girls helped the poorer people in the village. But Yvette left the rectory whenever she could. Sometimes she had tea with the wives of men who worked in the factories. She liked talking to the working men. Their world was very different from her own life in the rectory.

The months passed. Yvette went to lots of parties and dances. Sometimes friends came in their cars and took her to the city. But she never seemed to be really happy. At home, she was often angry, and she was rude to Aunt Cissie.

The girls hated inviting their friends to the rectory. There were only four rooms downstairs – the kitchen, the dining-room, the rector's study and the drawing-room. The drawing-room was the only room where a good hot fire was lit. So Granny always sat in the drawing-room. Whenever the girls brought their friends to the rectory, Granny was sitting in the drawing-room. The girls never felt comfortable and they could not relax when Granny was there.

Granny liked meeting people. She wanted to be introduced to all the girls' friends. She wanted to know who the young people were. She wanted to know where they came from and every detail of their lives. When Granny had this information, she took control of the conversation.

One afternoon, Lottie, Ella and Bob Framley – some of Yvette's friends – came to the house. A young man called Leo Wetherell came too. Granny had not met Leo before, so Yvette had to introduce him to her.

'Granny, this is Mr Wetherell.'

'Mr What-did-you-say?' shouted Granny. 'You must excuse me, I'm a little deaf. I can't hear properly.'

She held her hand towards Leo Wetherell and stared at him with her blind old eyes. Leo felt very uncomfortable.

'We want to go on a picnic[19] tomorrow,' said Ella. 'We're going to Bonsall Head, in Leo's car.'

There was a wonderful view from the top of Bonsall Head. From this high hill, you could see across the countryside for miles around.

'Did you say Bonsall Head?' asked Granny.

'Yes.'

There was a silence.

'Did you say that you were going in a car?' asked Granny.

'Yes,' said Yvette. 'In Mr Wetherell's car.'

'I hope that he's a good driver,' said Granny. 'The road to Bonsall Head is very dangerous.'

'Leo is a very good driver,' said Yvette.

'*Not* a very good driver?' said Granny.

'He *is* a very good driver!' shouted Yvette.

Then Aunt Cissie came into the room. Following her was the maid, who brought tea and a plate of little cakes. Several minutes later, Lucille returned from her job in the town. She was very tired and had black marks under her eyes. When she saw all the people in the drawing-room, she gave a little cry of surprise.

'You've never spoken about Mr Wetherell to me, have you, Lucille?' said Granny.

'I don't remember,' said Lucille.

'You can't have talked about him,' said Granny. 'I've never heard his name before.'

Yvette was eating the little cakes. Without thinking about anyone else, she took another cake from the plate. Aunt Cissie felt very angry with Yvette. She picked up her own plate, which had one small cake on it, and offered it to Yvette.

'Would you like my cake too?' she asked in a voice that was polite, but cold with anger.

'Oh, thanks!' said Yvette carelessly, taking Aunt Cissie's cake as well. Now she had two cakes on her plate. Aunt Cissie's face showed her feelings – feelings of hate. But Yvette did not notice[20] that anything was wrong.

Lucille and Yvette felt very tired when their friends left. The conversation between their friends and Granny had been very difficult. Yvette looked at her grandmother.

Granny looked like a kind, weak old lady, but she was very strong. She wanted to control other people by knowing everything about their lives. She was like a fat old toad[21] that Yvette had seen in the garden one day. The toad had sat by a bee-hive[22]. It had caught and eaten the bees as they came out of the hive.

Next day, the weather was dull and grey. The roads were wet and slippery because it had rained for several weeks. But the young people still wanted to drive up to Bonsall Head. There were two men in the group – Leo Wetherell and Bob Framley. And there were four girls – Lottie and Ella Framley, who were sisters, and Lucille and Yvette.

The young people all got into Leo's car. As he drove through the quiet villages, they all talked and sang songs. The car went along the road through dark trees, and then began the long slow climb up to Bonsall Head. At the top of the hill, there were no trees, there was only grass. On each side of the road there were low walls made of stone. Above the hills, the sky was dull and grey.

'Shall we stay here for a moment?' said Leo, stopping the car.

'Oh, yes!' cried the girls.

Leo turned off the engine and they all got out of the car. The view from the top of the Head was wonderful. All around, they could see hills and deep valleys. And towards the north, they saw a train moving slowly in the distance.

'Come on!' said Leo. 'Let's drive down to Amberdale and have some tea.'

The friends got back into the car and drove along the top of the Head. They were so high that it was like being on top of the world. Up here, it was cold and windy. The young people were silent, looking out across the stone walls.

Suddenly, ahead of them on the road, they saw a horse pulling a small green cart. The cart was driven by a man, and an old woman was walking by its side. Because the road was narrow, the car could not pass. Leo sounded the horn sharply and the man on the cart looked round. But the old woman walked on and did not turn her head.

Yvette's heart gave a jump. The man on the cart was a gipsy. He wore a dark green cap and a big red and yellow silk handkerchief around his neck. He sat on the cart in a comfortable, relaxed way.

'Get out of the way!' shouted Leo angrily.

The man pulled the horse's reins and the cart stopped. But it was still in the middle of the road and the car could not pass. So Leo had to stop the car too.

'Would the pretty young ladies like to have their fortunes told?' said the gipsy, laughing. 'Would they like to know what will happen to them in the future?'

The gipsy was very handsome, with black hair and a black moustache above very white teeth. His dark watchful eyes looked at Yvette's soft young face.

She looked into his eyes and felt a strange feeling of excitement. It was like a little flame in her heart. 'He's very strong,' she thought. 'He's stronger than I am!'

'Oh, yes!' cried the girls. 'Let's have our fortunes told!'

'But what about the time?' cried Leo. 'It's getting late.'

'It doesn't matter about the time,' said Lucille.

The gipsy jumped down lightly from the cart. He seemed a little over thirty years old and he was well-dressed. Beneath his black and green coat, he wore a dark green jumper, tight black trousers and black boots.

Now the young people saw that there was an old quarry on one side of the road. Many years ago, men had cut rock out of the ground and an opening had been made in the hill. There were three caravans in the quarry. The wall of rock rose high above the caravans, curving round towards the road. Grass grew between the rough stones on the ground. The quarry was a good place for the gipsies' winter camp[23].

The old gipsy woman went into one of the caravans. Two black-haired children looked out of the open door.

The gipsy gave a call and an old man came to take the horse from the cart. Then the gipsy went up the steps into the nearest caravan. At the same moment, a tall and handsome gipsy woman came down the steps. She had big gold rings in her ears and a pink headscarf over her black wavy hair. She wore a large green skirt. Her face was long and her eyes were bright and fierce, like a wolf[24].

'Which beautiful young lady wants to hear her fortune?' the woman asked. 'If she shows me her little hand, I can read her future.' The woman's eyes looked sharply from face to face.

Yvette, Lucille, Lottie and Ella all wanted the gipsy woman to tell them their fortunes. They agreed a price and the woman pulled two wooden stools from under a caravan.

The first girl, Lottie, sat down and the gipsy woman looked closely at her hand. She told Lottie about her future life. Yvette was the last girl to have her fortune told. The gipsy woman stared into the girl's face.

'I don't think that I want my fortune told,' Yvette said nervously[25].

'Are you afraid?' asked the woman. 'Do you have a secret? Would you like to go into the caravan, where nobody can hear?'

'Yes!' said Yvette. 'I'll go into the caravan.'

The gipsy woman called something to her husband. The gipsy man appeared at the top of the caravan steps. He was holding a small, black-haired baby in his arms. He came down the steps, looking at Yvette as he passed.

Yvette followed the woman up the steps of the caravan. At the top, she turned towards her friends.

'I won't be long,' she said.

Yvette's coat had soft, grey animal's fur around the collar. The collar was open, showing the white skin of her throat

Yvette followed the woman up the steps of the caravan. At the top, she turned towards her friends.

and her pale green dress. She knew that the gipsy man was looking at her as she entered his house.

Yvette's friends waited for a long time. It was getting dark and cold. At last the caravan door opened and Yvette came out. The gipsy woman followed her.

'Was I away a long time?' asked Yvette, not looking at anybody. 'I hope that you weren't bored! Wouldn't tea be nice! Shall we go?'

'You get in the car,' said Bob Framley. 'I'll pay.'

He gave some money to the gipsy woman. As Yvette got into the car, she also put some money into the woman's hand.

Leo started the engine and switched on the car's lights.

'Goodnight!' called Yvette.

As Leo turned the car onto the road, Lucille spoke to her sister. 'Yvette, tell us what the gipsy woman said to you.'

'Oh, nothing exciting,' said Yvette. 'Just the usual things. My future will include a dark man who means good luck, and a fair one who means bad luck. Someone in the family will die. I'll marry when I'm twenty-three. I'll have lots of money and love, and two children. That's all!'

At the rectory a few days later, there was a big quarrel between Yvette and Aunt Cissie. The quarrel was about Aunt Cissie's Window Fund.

Aunt Cissie had been collecting money to pay for a new, decorated glass window in the church. This window was to remember the men from the village who had died in the war. Aunt Cissie had asked Lucille and Yvette to collect money for the Window Fund too. She gave each of them a special money-box. The quarrel started when Aunt Cissie asked the girls for the money from their boxes. There was very little money in Yvette's box, only fifteen shillings.

'But some money must be missing. Where is the rest of it?' asked Aunt Cissie.

'Oh,' said Yvette carelessly. 'I borrowed[26] it.'

Aunt Cissie was very angry with Yvette. Yvette's father, the rector, was angry too.

'If you needed money, why didn't you tell me?' he said.

'I – I thought that it didn't matter,' said Yvette nervously. 'I needed to buy some things for myself. I can pay it back.'

'And what have you spent the money on?' her father asked.

'I can't remember,' said Yvette. 'I gave some of it away.'

Yvette's face was very pale. The rector was afraid that Yvette was becoming like his wife, Cynthia. *She* had behaved in the same careless way as Yvette. Now Yvette looked at him in the same way that Cynthia had done. Arthur Saywell felt guilty[27] and afraid.

'You must give the money back to the Window Fund,' he said coldly. 'I'll lend you some money now so that you can pay it back. In the future, if you can't trust yourself[28], don't touch money which isn't yours. You have not been honest. Dishonesty is a terrible thing.'

Yvette felt very bad. She knew that she had done wrong. She *had* been dishonest. She had taken money which was not hers and she had spent it. Why had she touched the money?

The rector paid the missing money to Aunt Cissie. But Aunt Cissie could not forgive Yvette. One night, when Yvette had gone to bed, her door opened softly. Aunt Cissie stood in the doorway of the bedroom, pushing her grey-green face forward. Terrified, Yvette sat up in her bed.

'Liar! Thief! Selfish little creature!' said Aunt Cissie in a voice full of hate. 'You're a selfish, greedy[29] little thief!'

Yvette opened her mouth to scream. But Aunt Cissie shut the door and disappeared. Yvette jumped out of bed and locked the bedroom door. She slowly got back into the bed and lay there, almost mad with fear.

'I wish that I were a gipsy,' she said to herself. 'I want to live in a camp, or a caravan. I never want to go into a house again. I hate this house. There's no fresh air here. I want to live my life freely. I want to live in the fresh air, like a gipsy.'

Then Yvette thought about the gipsy woman who had told her fortune. She remembered the woman's words.

'There's a dark man who never lived in a house. He loves you. Other people are treading on your heart. They will tread on your heart until you think that it's dead. But the dark man will blow the spark[30] *of life into fire again – a good fire.'*

Yvette hated the cold rectory. She liked the big dark gipsy woman who had gold rings in her ears. She liked the woman's strong hands. And the gipsy man! Yvette remembered the way that he had looked at her, and her body shook.

She had given two pounds from the Window Fund to the gipsy woman. She never told her father or Aunt Cissie this.

For several days, the weather was cold and wet. One afternoon, Lucille had a half day's holiday from her job in the city. The rector was writing in his study. Granny, Lucille and Yvette were in the drawing-room.

The girls were making a blue dress for Yvette. Granny was resting on the couch.

Yvette was sitting at the table, sewing her dress. The room was very untidy. There were small pieces of blue material everywhere and the scissors were lying on the floor. Yvette had placed a mirror on the top of the piano. But she had placed it in such a careless way that it could easily fall.

Aunt Cissie came into the room.

'This room is in a terrible mess[31]!' she said. 'You'll have to clear these things away, Yvette.'

'I'll clear everything away before we have tea,' Yvette replied. She got up and pulled the half-made blue dress over her head. But as she did so, she knocked the mirror off the top of the piano and it fell to the floor. Luckily the mirror did not break. But everybody got a terrible shock.

'Oh! She's smashed the mirror!' cried Aunt Cissie. 'It's broken!'

'Smashed a mirror! Which mirror? Who's smashed it?' said Granny sharply.

'I haven't smashed anything,' said Yvette calmly. 'It's all right. Anyway, it's my own mirror. I brought it from our home at the vicarage.'

'Don't break it in *this* house, wherever it came from,' said Granny. 'It's very unlucky to break a mirror. I don't want any bad luck brought to this house.'

'Oh, *I'm* not superstitious[32],' said Yvette. 'I don't believe that breaking a mirror will bring bad luck.'

'Yvette, will you please tidy this mess and put your things away,' said Aunt Cissie.

'It's really terrible to live with people who are always making a fuss[33] about small things!' cried Yvette angrily.

'Which people are you talking about?' said Aunt Cissie.

'You know who I'm talking about,' said Yvette. 'I'm talking about the people in this awful house.'

'Well,' said Granny. 'Thank goodness that there's nobody evil or mad, like your mother, in *our* family.'

For a second, there was a terrible silence. Then Lucille stood up quickly.

'You shut up!' she shouted at Granny.

Aunt Cissie angrily jumped towards Lucille and began to push her out of the room.

'Go to your bedroom!' she cried. 'Stay in your room until you've apologized to Granny. Say that you're sorry, then you can leave!'

'I shall *not* apologize!' shouted Lucille, and she left the room.

Yvette stood in the centre of the drawing-room. She was still wearing the half-made blue dress. She was shocked by what Lucille had said to Granny. But she was also very angry with Granny.

The rector came in. 'What's wrong?' he asked.

'Oh, nothing!' said Yvette carelessly. 'Lucille told Granny to shut up when she was saying something.'

'Lucille must learn to control her nerves[34],' said Granny. 'The mirror fell down, and it worried me. Yvette said something about superstitions and the people in this awful house. I said that the people in this house weren't evil or mad. Then Lucille told me to shut up. But it's only because of her nerves.'

Yvette was shocked. Granny was not telling the rector the truth. Granny had said that the girls' mother was evil and mad.

Aunt Cissie came back into the room. 'I've told Lucille not to come out of her room, until she apologizes,' she said.

'I don't want an apology,' said the old lady. 'Lucille's nerves made her behave like that.'

Yvette's body was shaking inside as she collected her thread, scissors and other sewing things.

She went up the stairs to see Lucille. Halfway up the stairs, there was a window. Yvette always looked out of this window, hoping to see someone on the road. The rectory was beside the River Papple. The road curved round the house, down to the bridge over the river, and on up to the village.

A horse, pulling a green cart, was coming down the road. It was driven by a man who was sitting on the front of the cart. He was wearing a green cap. It was the gipsy. At the back of the cart, there were metal pots and pans and long brushes.

The gipsy crossed the bridge, and passed along the road by the rectory wall. He looked up at the old stone house and saw Yvette standing at the window. He nodded his head to her.

Yvette was still wearing the blue dress, but it had no sleeves. Because she was a little cold, Yvette rubbed her hands along her pale arms.

The gipsy stopped at the white gate of the rectory, and jumped down from the cart. He took some brushes and other things from the back of the cart and turned towards the house. He looked up at Yvette as he opened the gate.

Yvette hurried to the bathroom and put on her other dress. Then she went downstairs to the drawing-room. The maid arrived there at the same time.

'Aunt Cissie,' Yvette said. 'There's a man selling brushes at the door. Shall I go and see him?'

'What kind of a man is he?' asked Aunt Cissie.

'A man with a cart,' said Yvette.

'A gipsy,' said the maid, coming into the drawing-room.

Aunt Cissie stood up. She wanted to see the gipsy herself.

The gipsy stood at the door, holding his brushes in one hand. From his other hand, shining metal objects were hanging – a saucepan, a candlestick and plates. He looked at Aunt Cissie with his large dark eyes.

'Do you want to buy anything today, lady?' he asked in a soft, quiet voice. Aunt Cissie saw that he was very handsome, so she did not close the door.

'This candlestick is lovely,' said Yvette. 'Did you make it?'

'Yes, lady!'

The gipsy looked at Yvette and his eyes showed his feelings for her. She knew that he wanted her. He desired[35] her. It made her feel weak.

Aunt Cissie went to show the rector the candlestick and Yvette was left alone with the gipsy.

'How is your wife?' she asked.

The man looked at Yvette and smiled. 'She's all right,' he said. 'When are you coming to the quarry again?' he asked in a low voice.

'Oh, I don't know,' said Yvette carelessly.

'Come on a Friday, when I'm there,' he said.

Yvette looked over the gipsy's shoulder at the road. She pretended[36] that she had not heard his words.

Aunt Cissie returned with money to buy the candlestick.

Yvette turned away and went upstairs. She stood beside the window on the stairs and looked onto the road. She did not want the gipsy to see her. She wanted to know if he had any power over her. Did he control her feelings and her mind?

She watched the gipsy walk through the white gate to the cart. He put his brushes and pans away and jumped onto the cart. Then he was gone.

'No, he hasn't any power over me!' said Yvette. And she went to see Lucille.

'Granny is sorry about what happened,' she said. 'Don't be angry. Let's go down to dinner. Come on, Lucille!'

When Friday came, Yvette thought all day about the quarry high up on Bonsall Head. She wanted to be there, among the caravans with the gipsies. But she did not go. She stayed at home and sewed her blue dress for a party the next day.

She danced with Leo Wetherell at the party.

'Why don't we get engaged, Yvette?' asked Leo.

Leo was an ordinary young man. But he was pleasant and kind, and he was rich. Yvette quite liked him. But she did not want to get engaged to him. What a silly idea! She did not think about Leo's feelings at all.

'Get engaged!' she said. 'But that's impossible.'

'Since those gipsies told your fortune, I've felt that I am the only one for you,' said Leo. 'And you are the only one for me.'

'Really!' said Yvette, very surprised. 'Really!'

'You felt the same thing, didn't you?' he said. 'Do you feel the same about me, as I feel about you?'

'What? Do you think that I want to get engaged?' she said. 'No. How could I dream of such an impossible thing?'

The musicians began to play again and people stood up to dance. Leo looked at Yvette.

'I won't dance any more,' she said. 'But do go and ask

somebody else to dance with you.'

Leo stood up angrily and walked away from her. Yvette watched the young men dancing. Then suddenly a picture of the gipsy came into her mind. She saw his face, his straight nose, his smiling lips. She saw his black eyes, which seemed to look deep into a dark, secret place inside her.

The gipsy was so different from the young men around her. Yvette did not want any of *them*. When Leo smiled at her, his smile did not make a flame burn in her heart.

The next week, it rained again. But when Friday came, it was sunny and cold. Yvette told her family that she was going for a ride on her bicycle. But she did not tell them that she was going to visit the gipsies' camp.

It was February and the sun was not strong enough to melt the ice on the ground. But the sun made Yvette think of spring. Her body was warm from cycling, but her hands were very cold. She was not wearing gloves.

The horse and cart were not in the camp. The gipsy man was sitting on the ground, making a metal bowl. He was not wearing a coat or a cap. The sun shone on his black hair and green jumper. An old woman was cooking some food in an iron pot over the fire. Three small children were playing near her. The man looked up as Yvette got off her bicycle.

'How are you all?' she asked politely.

'All right. Do you want to sit down for a minute?' he said, pulling a wooden stool from under a caravan.

Yvette went to the fire to warm her hands near the flames.

'Are you cooking dinner?' she asked the old woman.

'Yes,' the woman replied. 'Dinner for him. And for the children.' She pointed at the three black-eyed, black-haired children. They were staring at Yvette. The gipsies, their caravans and everything in the camp was clean and tidy. The children began to play again like little wild animals.

'Are they your children?' Yvette asked the gipsy man.

He looked straight into her eyes, and nodded.

'Where's your wife?'

'She's taken the cart, to try and sell things. I don't go selling things. I make them, but I don't go selling them. Not often.'

Yvette sat down on the stool. 'You said that you would be here on a Friday,' she said. 'And the weather was fine today. So I came this way.'

'It's a very fine day!' said the gipsy. 'Do you want some dinner? There's meat with some beans in it.'

'Yes, please. I'll have just a little,' said Yvette.

'Do you want to come up into the caravan and wash your hands?'

'No, thank you,' she said. 'They're clean.'

They ate the food, sitting round the fire. The children sat on the ground, eating beans and meat with a spoon or their fingers. The gipsy man was silent. Then the old woman made some coffee.

Yvette took off her hat and shook her short, brown hair in the sunshine.

'How many children do you have?' Yvette asked suddenly.

'Five, I think,' replied the gipsy slowly, looking up into her eyes. He held a cup of coffee towards her and she took it. She knew that he was sitting there silently, like a shadow[37].

Yvette's hair fell across her face as she put her lips to the hot cup. She felt very weak, as if the gipsy had complete power over her. And as he drank his own coffee, he looked at her.

'Do you want to go to my caravan now, and wash your hands?' he said.

'Yes, I think so,' she said.

He got up quietly. Then he spoke a few words to the old woman and climbed up the steps to his caravan. Yvette stood still at the bottom of the steps.

Suddenly they heard the sound of a car. A big, powerful car passed the quarry, then stopped. The gipsy came down the steps of the caravan again.

'Put on your hat,' he said to Yvette.

Yvette went back to the stool by the fire. The gipsy picked up his tools and began working on the metal bowl again.

'May we warm our hands at the camp fire?' said a voice.

A small woman came towards the fire. She was wearing a fur coat, but her body was shaking with the cold. A large, fair-haired man was following her. He was tall and strong, with a body like an athlete's.

The woman sat at the fire and held her hands towards the warm flames. The gipsy was still making his metal bowl. The big blond man went over to him.

'We're on our honeymoon[38],' the woman said to Yvette. 'But it's a honeymoon before we're married!'

'Really!' said Yvette. She was surprised.

'Yes! Have you heard of Simon Fawcett?' the woman asked. She was talking about a rich, well-known engineer[39] in northern England. 'Well, I'm Mrs Fawcett. My husband is divorcing me. As soon as the divorce is complete, I'm going to marry this man – Major Eastwood.'

She turned round and looked at the large blond man who was talking to the gipsy. Then she looked at the gipsy. Her big brown eyes shone. 'He's a handsome man!' she said.

'Yes, quite handsome!' said Yvette.

'Are you cycling?' asked the woman, looking at Yvette's bicycle by the caravan.

'Yes. I'm going down to Papplewick,' replied Yvette. 'My father is the rector of Papplewick.'

Major Eastwood came and stood by the fire. 'We were talking about the war,' he said. 'I thought that I remembered that man's face. He served in my regiment[40]. He took care of the horses. He was excellent.'

'Why don't you come with us in our car?' said the woman

to Yvette. 'We live in Scoresby. That's near Papplewick. We can tie your bicycle onto the back of the car.'

'Thank you. I think that I will,' said Yvette.

'It's going to snow,' said the woman, looking up at the cold, grey sky. She closed the collar of her fur coat around her neck.

'Are you going back in the car?' the gipsy asked, looking at Yvette.

'Yes,' she replied. 'The weather changes very quickly.'

Yvette did not know what the gipsy was thinking. But she was not very interested. She was more interested in Mrs Fawcett. This woman had left her rich husband and had run away with Major Eastwood, a poor man who was five or six years younger than her.

'Well, goodbye!' said Mrs Fawcett to the gipsy. 'Thank you for the warm fire.'

'Fire is free for everyone,' said the gipsy.

'Goodbye!' said Yvette. 'I hope that it doesn't snow.'

'We don't worry about a little snow,' said the gipsy.

And Yvette followed the woman in the fur coat to the car.

Yvette was excited about her new friends. She called them the Eastwoods. They were renting[41] a small cottage near the hills. Mrs Eastwood was thirty-six. She had two children, who were both more than twelve years old. She had left them with her husband. But Mr Fawcett had agreed that the children could live with their mother when the divorce was complete.

The Eastwoods were a strange couple. Mrs Eastwood was a tiny woman, with big eyes and curly black hair. Major Charles Eastwood looked completely different. He was a big young man with bright blond hair and light grey eyes. He looked like a great, pale bird of winter.

The Eastwoods invited Yvette for a meal at their cottage. Yvette thought that they were very unusual and interesting people. She told Lucille about her new friends, but she did not tell the rector, Granny, or Aunt Cissie. She knew that they would ask her a lot of questions.

'But I don't want you to visit us if your father doesn't know about our friendship,' said Mrs Eastwood.

'I'm sure that he won't worry,' said Yvette.

Yvette talked about many things with the Eastwoods. On one visit, they talked about love and marriage.

'Don't you want to fall in love and get married?' asked Mrs Eastwood.

'No, not really,' said Yvette.

'But don't you know what love is?' said Mrs Eastwood in surprise. 'Is there no man who makes you feel different?'

'I don't think so,' said Yvette. 'Except – yes! There is *one* man who makes me feel different. The gipsy.'

'What gipsy?'

'The one who was a soldier and cared for the horses in Major Eastwood's regiment in the war.'

'You're not in love with him!' said Mrs Eastwood in a shocked voice.

'Well!' said Yvette. 'I don't know. He's the only man who makes me feel different. He really is! He looked at me in a different way from any other man. He looked as if he really desired me – really wanted me.'

'What a horrible man!' cried Mrs Eastwood.

'Do you think that he *shouldn't* look at me?' asked Yvette.

'No! He certainly should not!' cried Mrs Eastwood.

'But it was rather wonderful. It really was!' said Yvette. 'And nothing like that has happened in my life.'

'I think,' said the Major, 'that desire for a woman is the most wonderful thing.'

'Do you think that the gipsy is special?' asked Yvette.

'If I were you, I should know,' said the Major.

'But she can't possibly marry him and live in a caravan!' said Mrs Eastwood in a shocked voice.

'I never said that she should marry him,' said Major Eastwood.

'And she shouldn't have a love affair,' said Mrs Eastwood.

Major Eastwood thought for several moments.

'That gipsy was the best man that we had who worked with horses,' he said. 'He became ill and almost died. I almost died too. I was buried for twenty hours under snow. I was only found by accident[42].'

'Oh,' said Yvette. 'Life is so terrible.'

Yvette had thought that her father would not worry about her friendship with the Eastwoods. But when the rector heard about them, he was very angry.

'I've heard that your new friends are the half-divorced Mrs Fawcett and her boyfriend, Eastwood,' he said.

'They're very nice,' said Yvette. 'They'll be married in about a month. I like them very much. They both seem such honest people.'

'You've got a strange idea about honesty,' said the rector. 'Eastwood is a young man who lives with a woman older than himself. He lives on her money. The woman has left her home and her children! And you seem to know them very well. Where did you meet them?'

'I was riding my bicycle,' said Yvette. 'I met them on the road. They came along in their car and we started to talk.'

'And how many times have you visited them?'

'I've been to their cottage in Scoresby twice.'

The rector looked at Yvette with hate in his eyes. He remembered his wife, Cynthia. Cynthia had behaved like Mrs Eastwood. Cynthia had left *him* and run away with a younger, poor man. His daughter liked the Eastwoods. She did not think that their behaviour was wrong. Was Yvette becoming like Cynthia?

'Yvette, why do you make friends with people like the Eastwoods?' he said. 'Aren't there enough good people in the world for you? You must stop this kind of behaviour. Or you will have to live with mad, bad people.'

Yvette's face became pale. She felt cold with fear.

'But why?' she said. 'What have I done? Is it a very bad thing, to be friends with the Eastwoods?'

'Don't say any more,' said the rector. 'I'll kill you before you go down the same bad road as your mother.'

Yvette looked at her father. The skin of his face was pale yellow, and his eyes were mad with fear, anger and hate. Yvette felt very cold and lonely. There was a terrible silence.

'Are you saying that I can't be a friend of the Eastwoods?' she asked again.

'You can be their friend, if you wish,' said the rector. 'But if you are, you cannot be with your Granny, your Aunt Cissie, and Lucille. You have to choose between clean people like your Granny, and people who are unclean in their bodies and minds.'

There was another silence.

'All right,' said Yvette at last. 'I'll write to the Eastwoods. I'll say that you don't want me to know them.'

She walked quietly out of the room and wrote a note to Mrs Eastwood.

Dear Mrs Eastwood,

Daddy isn't happy that I'm visiting you. So you'll understand that I can no longer come to Scoresby. I'm very sorry.

After she had sent the note, Yvette felt empty. Her life was dull. Her home was cold and loveless. She thought about the gipsy again. She wanted him to hold her in his arms and keep her safe from her father. Her feelings for her father had changed. She still liked him, but she no longer loved him. His words had hurt her very much. And she began to hate Granny. Whenever she saw the fat, blind old woman sitting in the drawing-room, she thought of a great toad.

After she had sent the note, Yvette saw the gipsy twice. Once he came to the house with things to sell. She stood by the window on the stairs and watched him. But she did not go downstairs and talk to him.

The second time that Yvette saw the gipsy, she met him by accident. It was March, and the weather was sunny. Brightly coloured spring flowers were growing in the woods and on the hills and fields. Yvette was cycling along the road. She saw the gipsy coming out of a stone cottage. His horse and the green cart were standing in the road. He returned to the cart with some of his brushes.

Yvette got off her bicycle. As soon as she saw him, she loved him. She knew that she loved the way that he moved. She loved his face as he turned, silently, towards her. She felt that she knew him better than she knew anybody. She knew him better than her sister, Lucille. She felt that she belonged to the gipsy forever.

'Have you made anything new?' she asked, looking at the things on his cart.

'I don't think so,' he said.

When the gipsy looked at her, there was still desire in his eyes. But now the desire was less strong.

'The old gipsy dreamed something about you,' he said.

'Did she?' cried Yvette, very interested. 'What did she tell you?'

'She said, "Be braver in your body, or your luck will leave you." And then she said, "Listen for the voice of water."'

'What does that mean?' asked Yvette in surprise.

'I asked her that question,' the gipsy said. 'She says that she doesn't know.'

Then he was silent, as he looked at her soft face.

'All right,' she said. 'I don't understand the words now, but perhaps I'll understand them in the future.' She looked at him with clear, shining eyes.

'Aren't you coming to the quarry again?' he said.

'Perhaps I'll come, sometime,' she said.

'It's spring!' he said, smiling and looking round at the

sun. 'We're going to pack up our camp soon, and go away.'

'All right,' Yvette said. 'Perhaps I *will* visit before you go. I'll come and say goodbye to your wife, and the old woman who sent me the message.'

But Yvette did not visit the gipsies' camp at the quarry. She went out with her friends to parties, and she danced with Leo Wetherell. She wanted to go and say goodbye to the gipsies. But she did not.

———

It was Friday afternoon. The weather was fine, and the sun shone brightly on the yellow flowers in the rectory garden. The River Papple was very full of water. The water rushed quickly and noisily under the stone bridge. It was unusual for the river to have so much water in it.

Yvette felt very lazy. She did not want to do anything. She walked in the garden by the river. The rector had gone out, and Lucille was at work. Granny was inside the house with Aunt Cissie.

Yvette sat on a wooden seat which was only a few feet above the river. She thought about the gipsies.

'The gipsies' camp is a better home for me, than here in the rectory,' she thought.

Yvette looked again at the river. The brown water was rushing past the garden extremely quickly. She remembered the message from the old gipsy: '*Listen for the voice of water.*'

Yvette heard a voice calling her name. Aunt Cissie was standing by a door of the house, waving her hand.

'Yvette! I'm going to the village!' Cissie shouted. 'I won't be away for long. Don't forget that Granny is alone.'

'All right!' Yvette shouted back.

The sun was beginning to go down. It was past five o'clock. Yvette would have to go back into the rectory soon. Once again, she would have to be in those horrible rooms with Granny. She walked by the river. She did not want to go inside the ugly house.

Suddenly she heard the sharp noise of a horse and cart on the road. And somebody was shouting. It was the gipsy. He was waving his hands at her wildly, and shouting.

Yvette turned and looked behind her. At that moment, she heard a sound like the roar of a great and dangerous animal. A huge wall of water was coming around the bend of the river and rushing down towards her.

The gipsy was shouting and running across the garden. He pulled her arm and screamed, 'Run!'

The huge wave of water swept Yvette off her feet. The gipsy pulled her towards the house. He was trying to take her to the steps that led up to the front door. But before they reached the steps, another wave hit them and covered their heads. The water was as cold as ice. The gipsy pulled Yvette up again.

'Go to the steps!' he shouted in Yvette's ear, pushing her in front of him.

At last, they reached the steps of the house. Another wall of water came roaring to the house, and the walls shook. The gipsy pushed open the door and they were swept inside.

The water filled the hall. Suddenly they saw Granny come out of the drawing-room. She felt the water all around her legs, and opened her mouth in a cry of fear.

Yvette climbed up the stairs. Water poured from her hair and clothes. The gipsy followed her, his wet black hair over his eyes.

From the top of the stairs, they stared at the flood which rushed through the hall below them. Yvette saw Granny's body in the water. Her old face was purple and her mouth opened and closed. But no sound came out. She was trying to hold onto the stairs with one hand. Yvette saw the old woman's gold wedding ring shining on her finger.

Another wave of water struck the house and there was a strange cracking noise. Yvette reached the door of her bedroom. The water moved below them like a wild brown

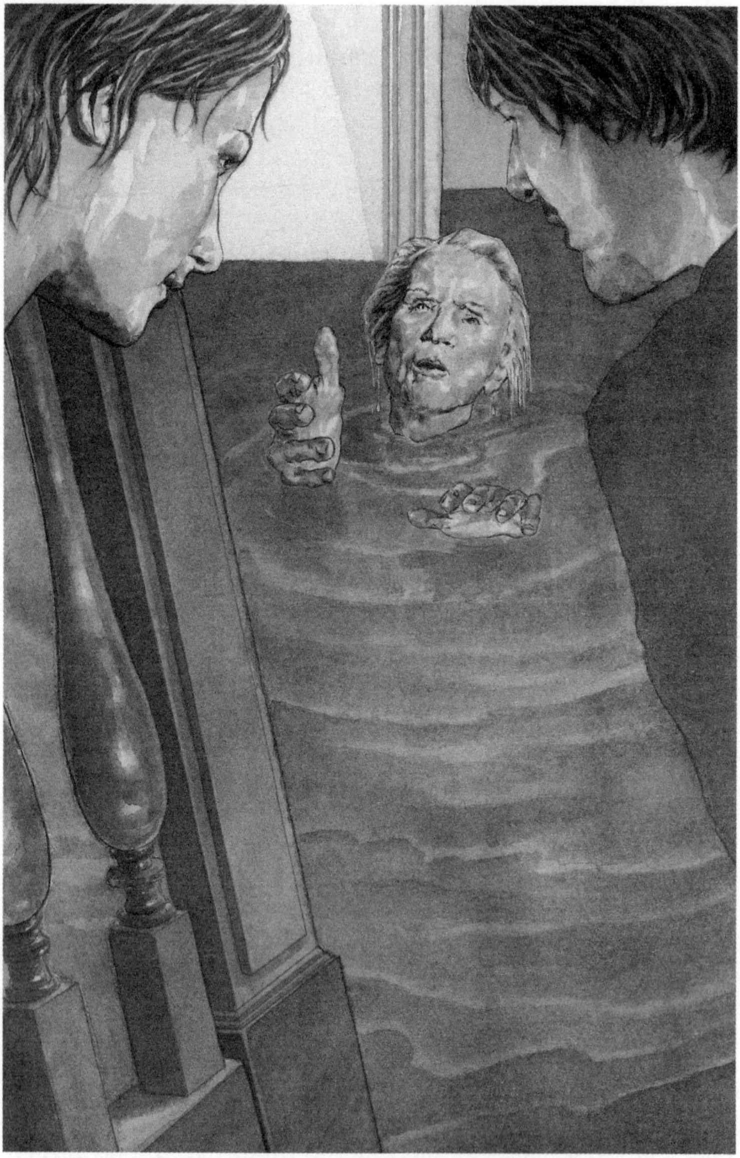

Yvette saw Granny's body in the water.

sea. They felt the house begin to move.

'The house is going to fall!' shouted the gipsy. 'Where is the chimney[43]? The chimney is strong. It won't fall. We must get near the chimney. Then we'll be safe.'

'Come in here! In here!' said Yvette.

The chimney was in one wall of Yvette's bedroom. They went into the room and the gipsy looked out of the window. Outside, between the house and the hill, there was a sea of water. Broken trees and other things were being swept around in the wild brown flood.

There was a terrible noise from somewhere in the house. Walls were falling.

'It's all right,' said the gipsy. 'This room is safe.' He pointed to the chimney. 'Look, the chimney is strong. It's like a tower. But we must get warm. Take off your wet clothes and get into the bed. I'll rub you with a towel[44] so that you can get dry. I'll dry myself too.'

The gipsy pulled off his wet clothes. He took a towel and began to rub his cold wet body quickly.

Yvette took off her dress. Her body was shaking. The gipsy went to the door and looked out.

The sky was quite dark now. The end of the house that was nearest to the river had gone. The water had swept the walls away. The stairs had disappeared too.

'It's all right! The water isn't rising any higher,' said the gipsy. 'Get into the bed. Lie under the blankets.'

Yvette pulled the sheets and blankets over her head. Her body was shaking with cold. Suddenly she uncovered her head and looked at the gipsy.

'M-make me warm!' she cried. Her teeth were snapping together between each word. 'I w-will d-die from the c-cold.'

The gipsy nodded his head and held her in his arms. His body was shaking too. He held her body tightly against his own body. Slowly, they began to feel warm again. At last they slept.

The next day, the sun was shining in a beautiful blue sky. The bridge had broken and disappeared. But the water had stopped rising. Most of the rectory had been destroyed in the flood. The south-west corner of the house was now a great pile of mud and stones.

By midday, men from Papplewick village arrived at the rectory. They used ladders[45] to get across the river to the house. In the kitchen, they found Granny's body among the mud, trees and broken furniture.

Then more villagers came running down the hill. They had a message from the old gipsy. He had said that his son had been near the rector's house. He had seen Yvette at the top of the house.

Everyone began to search for Yvette. The men put a long ladder up to the window of her bedroom. A policeman from Papplewick climbed up the ladder and broke the glass of the window. He saw Yvette lying in the bed, asleep. The noise of the breaking glass woke her. She sat up suddenly, holding a blanket around her.

The policeman shouted to the people below, 'Miss Yvette's in bed!'

'Don't be frightened, miss,' he said to Yvette. 'Don't worry any more. You're safe now.'

Yvette did not understand. Was the policeman talking about the gipsy? Where was her gipsy? What had happened to him? He had gone! And a policeman was looking into the room!

'If you get dressed, miss, we'll take you down to safe ground,' said the policeman. 'You can't stay here. The house will probably fall.'

The policeman turned his head away and waited. Yvette took some clothes from a cupboard and put them on. The gipsy's wet clothes were no longer on the floor. There was just a wet mark on the carpet. Yvette called to the policeman.

'We must get out of the house as soon as possible, miss,' he said. 'The house may fall.'

'Really!' said Yvette calmly. 'Is it as bad as that?'

She heard shouts from outside. She went to the window and looked out. There, below, was her father. The rector's arms were wide open and tears were running down his face.

'I'm all right, Daddy,' Yvette said calmly. And tears began to run down her own face.

'Don't cry, miss, don't cry!' said the policeman. 'The rector has lost his mother, but he's very thankful that you're alive.'

'Is Granny drowned?' asked Yvette.

'I'm afraid that she is dead, poor lady!' said the policeman. 'Can you go down the ladder, miss?'

Yvette looked at the ladder. It did not look safe. But then she remembered the words of the old gipsy: '*Be braver in the body.*'

'Oh, yes!' she said.

At the bottom of the ladder, she ran into her father's arms.

Later, a car took Yvette and her father to the Framleys' house. Lucille and Aunt Cissie were waiting there. Lucille cried when she saw that her sister was safe. Even Aunt Cissie was happy that Yvette was safe.

'I can't cry about Granny, now that Yvette is alive!' Aunt Cissie said.

The flood had happened because of a great reservoir[46], five miles from the rectory. The reservoir contained a huge amount of water. But the wall of the reservoir had become weak and had suddenly burst.

The water had rushed through the broken wall, and down to the village, in a great flood.

Yvette did not tell anyone that the gipsy had been in her bedroom. She only said that he had taken her inside the house. She said that she had climbed up the stairs alone.

But Yvette knew that the gipsy had escaped. The old

gipsy had come to the village to get the horse and cart. He had said that his son was safe.

'We should thank the gipsy who saved Yvette's life,' said Lucille.

The rector and his daughters went to the quarry. But it was empty. The gipsies had packed up their camp and left.

That night, Yvette lay in her bed and thought about everything that had happened. There was a deep pain in her heart.

'Oh, I love him! I love him! I love him!' she said to herself.

Some time later, Yvette received a short letter.

Dear Miss,

I saw in the paper that you were all right. So was I. I hope that I'll see you again one day. I came that day to say goodbye, but the water gave me no time.

Your servant,

Joe Boswell

For the first time, Yvette realized that the gipsy had a name.

THE LOVELY LADY

Pauline Attenborough was seventy-two years old, but she looked much younger. When a soft light shone on her, she could look as young as thirty. She had a lovely figure and face, and her nose was a very good shape. Only her big grey eyes made her look older.

Pauline had left her husband, Ronald, many years ago. Pauline and Ronald had had two sons, Henry and Robert. Henry, the older son, had died when Robert was only ten. Now Robert was thirty-two. He lived with his mother and worked as a lawyer in London. Robert Attenborough did not earn very much money, but this was not a problem. His mother was a rich woman.

Pauline's niece, Ciss, also lived in the house. Her father, Ronald Attenborough's brother, had died five years ago. Ciss had no money or home of her own. She needed a place to live. So she depended[47] on her Aunt Pauline.

Ciss was a big young woman, with dark hair and eyes. She was very shy[48]. She was in love with her cousin, Robert, but she had never told him this. Robert was also very shy. He had no confidence in himself.

Pauline, Robert and Ciss lived together quietly, in a lovely house about twenty-five miles from London. The house was surrounded by pleasant gardens. It was the perfect house and the perfect life for Pauline. Every day, Robert went to work in London. Then when he came home, the three of them – Pauline, Robert and Ciss – ate dinner together.

During dinner, there were always candles on the table. Pauline liked candles because the soft candlelight made her look young and beautiful. The soft light shone on the skin of her bare arms and the soft material of her dress. Pauline shone with happiness. She looked like a beautiful woman of only thirty-two or thirty-three.

After dinner, they had coffee in the warm drawing-room. The room was full of lovely furniture. For many years, Pauline had collected furniture and beautiful, unusual pictures from many different countries. She had sold these things to museums for a lot of money. This had made her a rich woman.

Pauline, Robert and Ciss chatted[49] together pleasantly. Their conversation was always simple and bright. Then at half past eight, Ciss carried the tray of coffee things out of the room. Robert always stayed and continued chatting to his mother. He always listened to everything that she said.

At the side of the house, there was a large courtyard[50]. Ciss had a flat[51] just across the courtyard, above the old coach-house and stables. Several years ago, a carriage and horses had been kept in these buildings. Now Robert kept his car in the coach-house.

Ciss did not always go to her flat after dinner. In summer, she sometimes sat outside in the large garden. She listened to Pauline's laughter coming from the drawing-room. In winter, Ciss put on a thick coat and walked through the garden and down to the little bridge over the stream. She liked to hear the water running under the bridge. She would look back at the lighted windows of the drawing-room, where Pauline and Robert were so happy together.

Ciss loved Robert. 'I believe that Pauline wants Robert to marry me when she dies,' she thought. 'But Robert is very shy. Perhaps his mother won't die for many years. By that time, it will be too late. Robert will be just an empty man who never enjoyed his life.'

Sometimes Ciss stayed in the dark garden until about ten o'clock, when she saw the light go on in Pauline's bedroom. Robert usually stayed in the drawing-room for another hour, then he would go to bed too. Ciss, standing in the garden, wanted to go to him. She wanted to say, 'Oh, Robert! This is all wrong!' But she could not do this because Aunt Pauline would hear. So she went to her own rooms.

In the mornings, Robert went to London at about nine o'clock. Pauline rested in bed. She came downstairs at lunchtime. Sometimes she did not leave her bedroom until tea-time. But she always looked fresh and young.

Pauline always had a rest in the afternoons. When the sun shone, she liked to lie outside and bathe in the warm sun. Behind the stables, there was a second, smaller courtyard which was surrounded by trees. The sun shone right down into this little courtyard, so it was a perfect place for sunbathing. Here, Ciss put a chair for Pauline to lie on, a large umbrella and blankets. If the sun became too hot, Pauline could lie in the shade of the umbrella.

One afternoon, Ciss decided to sunbathe too. She found a ladder and climbed up onto the flat roof of the stables. Then she lay down on a blanket in one corner of the roof. The sun shone brightly here and it was very hot. Ciss was above Aunt Pauline, who lay in the little courtyard below. But Pauline did not know that Ciss was on the roof above her.

It was lovely, lying in the warm sun and air. The warmth of the sun on her legs and arms made Ciss feel comfortable and relaxed. Suddenly she heard a voice speaking softly and her heart jumped with fear and shock.

'No, Henry dear!' said the voice. 'It was not my fault[52] that you died instead of marrying Claudia.'

The voice did not sound human. Where was it coming from? There must be someone on the roof! Ciss lifted her head and looked around. But there was nobody on the roof with her.

Suddenly she heard the soft voice again.

'No, darling! I said that you would be tired of her in six months! I warned you, and it was true. I couldn't do anything more. And you died without ever knowing me again.'

The voice was silent. Ciss lay on her blanket. It was a beautiful summer afternoon. Did the voice belong to a ghost? Ciss hated the idea of ghosts, spirits and magic.

Then she heard a deep sigh[53] and the strange voice spoke again.

'Ah, well, a heart must feel pain! But it wasn't my fault, dear. It is better for a heart to feel pain, rather than break from sorrow. And Robert could marry poor, boring Ciss tomorrow, if he wanted to. But he doesn't care about her.'

Ciss sat up quickly. She was very surprised. It was Aunt Pauline talking! It *must* be Aunt Pauline! Where was she? And how was Ciss hearing her strange whispers? Aunt Pauline must be lying right below her. And she must be using a trick to make her voice sound strange. Aunt Pauline was trying to frighten her! Ciss was still afraid, but she was now thinking more clearly.

Ciss lay down again. She knew the story of Henry, Robert's older brother. Henry had been in love with Claudia, a beautiful young actress. But his mother had been against Claudia and had laughed at Henry. Henry had become ill with a brain disease and died at the age of twenty-two.

'I think that I should get up now,' the voice was saying. 'I've had enough sun. A woman might live forever if she has enough sun, love and good food. I truly believe a good life will make me live forever.'

'That is certainly Aunt Pauline's voice,' Ciss said to herself. 'How horrible! I'm hearing Aunt Pauline's thoughts.'

Ciss turned and looked down in front of her. She was staring at a hole in the corner of the roof. The lead gutter, the pipe for taking away the rainwater, went down into this hole. The water then came out of the rain pipe, near the ground. Suddenly a sigh and a whisper came out of the hole.

'Ah well, Pauline! Get up. You've had enough sun today.'

Now Ciss understood. Aunt Pauline was lying below her and the rain pipe was carrying her voice up to the roof! Aunt Pauline was speaking her thoughts aloud. She did not know that the sound of her voice was going up to the roof.

So Aunt Pauline was feeling guilty about Henry's death. He had died and she thought that it was her fault. Ciss believed that Pauline had loved her big, handsome son Henry, more than she loved Robert. Henry's death had been a terrible shock for Pauline. She only loved Robert because Henry was dead.

Ciss put on her clothes, picked up her blanket, and carefully climbed down the ladder. As she went down, she heard her aunt calling, 'All right, Ciss!' The lovely lady had finished sunbathing. She was returning to the house.

Ciss went into the small courtyard. She picked up Pauline's blankets and the chair and put them in the house. Then she looked for the opening of the rain pipe. She found it in the corner of two walls of the stable building. The mouth of the rain pipe was almost hidden by the leaves of a plant on the wall. When Pauline sat in her chair and turned her face to the wall, her mouth would be near to the rain pipe. Ciss had heard her aunt's voice. No ghosts, spirits, or magic had made the voice.

That evening, after they had drunk their coffee, Pauline stood up. 'The sun has made me so sleepy today,' she said. 'I shall go to bed now. You two sit and chat.'

When Pauline had gone to bed, Ciss turned towards Robert. 'Do you remember your brother, Henry?' she asked him.

Robert looked at her in surprise. 'Yes, very well,' he said.

'What was he like?' asked Ciss.

'Tall and handsome, with soft brown hair like mother,' Robert said. 'Women liked him. Henry was very happy and clever.'

'Did he love your mother?'

'Very much,' Robert said. 'She loved him too – more than she loves me.'

'Robert,' Ciss said. 'Do you like me?'

The mouth of the rain pipe was almost hidden by the leaves of a plant on the wall.

Ciss saw Robert's face become pale.

'Yes,' Robert said. 'I like you very much.'

'Will you kiss me? Nobody ever kisses me,' Ciss said.

Robert looked at his cousin with fear in his eyes. Then he stood up and kissed her gently on the cheek. Ciss held Robert's hand and pressed it against her breast.

'Come and sit with me in the garden,' she said.

'But what about mother?' he said. He was nervous and shy.

Ciss smiled a little and looked into his eyes. Suddenly Robert's face became red. A few minutes later, she left him and went to her flat.

The sunny weather continued. It was now July. Every afternoon, Pauline sunbathed in the small courtyard. And Ciss lay on the roof above the stables, listening. But the sound of Pauline's voice did not come up the pipe again.

After dinner in the evenings, Ciss waited in the garden. She saw the light go on in her aunt's bedroom. She saw the lights go out in the drawing-room. She waited, but Robert did not come into the garden. Then one night, he came out and walked towards her. Ciss stood up and walked softly over the grass to him.

'Don't speak,' Robert whispered.

They stood together, looking up at the stars in the dark sky.

'How can I ask you to love me?' he said. 'And how can I marry? I haven't made much money. And I can't ask my mother for money.'

'Then don't worry about marrying yet,' Ciss said. 'But do love me a little.'

Robert gave a short laugh. 'It's hard to begin,' he said.

They sat down and he held her hand. At last she said goodnight, stood up, and went indoors.

The next day, Ciss lay on the roof, sunbathing. Suddenly she heard her aunt's voice from the hole in the lead gutter.

First Pauline spoke in Italian, then she spoke in English.

'No, Robert dear,' said Pauline's voice. 'You will never be the same kind of man as your father. But you look like him. Mauro was a wonderful lover. Mauro! Mauro! How you loved me!'

The voice stopped speaking. Ciss realized that her aunt had a secret. Pauline's husband, Ronald, had not been Robert's father! Robert's father had been an Italian man called Mauro.

'I'm disappointed with you, Robert,' continued Pauline's voice. 'Your father was a priest, but he was the best lover in the world. You are like a cold fish. And Ciss is like a cat who is trying to catch you.'

Ciss suddenly put her mouth near the hole in the rain pipe and spoke. 'Leave Robert alone!' she said in a deep voice. 'Don't kill him too.'

There was a silence. The hot afternoon sun shone on the flat roof of the stables. Ciss listened, with her heart beating quickly. At last she heard her aunt Pauline whisper the words, 'Did someone speak?'

Ciss spoke again into the hole of the lead gutter.

'You killed me,' she said in a deep, terrible voice. 'Don't kill Robert too!'

'Ah!' said Pauline, giving a little cry. 'Who's speaking?'

'Henry!' said Ciss in the same, deep voice.

There was silence again.

'I didn't kill you, Henry,' said Pauline. 'No! No! Henry, it wasn't my fault. I loved you, my dearest boy. I only wanted to help you.'

'You killed me!' Ciss said in the deep voice. 'Now, let Robert live. Let him go! Let him marry!'

'Henry!' said Pauline. 'Are you a ghost? Have you come to punish[54] me for your death?'

'YES! I HAVE COME TO PUNISH YOU!' said Ciss in a terrible, frightening voice.

She was very angry with Pauline. She felt that her anger was going down the rain pipe to her aunt. At the same time, she almost laughed. This was a very funny conversation!

Ciss lay and listened. No sound came from the rain pipe. The afternoon had become cooler. Yellow and grey clouds had covered the sun. There was a roar of thunder. A storm was coming. Ciss dressed quickly, went down the ladder, and ran to the corner of the stables.

'Aunt Pauline!' she called. 'Did you hear thunder?'

'Y-yes! I am going indoors,' her aunt replied in a weak voice. 'Don't wait for me.'

Ciss watched her aunt go inside the house. The sky was growing darker. Ciss took the blankets and the chair and hurried inside.

Then the storm began. Pauline did not come downstairs to tea because she did not like thunder. Robert did not arrive home until after tea. By this time, the rain was pouring down.

Ciss went to her flat and got ready for dinner. She put on a pretty white dress and fastened some white flowers at her breast. When she went into the drawing-room, Robert was waiting. He was standing by the drawing-room window and listening to the rain falling. He now had a different look on his face as he watched her.

The drawing-room was lit by the soft light of a table lamp. Ciss walked towards the bookshelves near the door. When she heard the door opening softly, Ciss suddenly turned on the switch of the ceiling light. Her aunt, wearing a black dress, stood in the doorway. The strong, hard light showed her face clearly. Pauline was wearing make-up, but her face looked old and full of hate.

'Oh, Aunt!' cried Ciss.

'Mother, you look like a little old lady!' said Robert in a shocked voice.

'Aren't we going to eat dinner?' asked Pauline angrily.

... her face looked old and full of hate.

Pauline sat at the table, getting angrier and angrier. She looked very, very old and very ugly.

Ciss and Robert watched each other. He was very shocked by his mother's face. Pauline ate her dinner quickly, like a hungry dog. As soon as they had finished eating, she ran towards the stairs. Robert and Ciss followed her from the room.

'You pour the coffee. I hate it,' said the old woman quickly. 'I'm going to bed! Goodnight!'

There was silence. At last Robert said, 'I'm afraid that Mother isn't well. She must see a doctor.'

'Yes,' said Ciss.

The rest of the evening passed in silence. Robert and Ciss stayed in the drawing-room. A fire was lit. Outside, cold rain was falling.

At about ten o'clock, the door opened and Pauline came into the room. She shut the door and came to the fire. Then she looked at Robert and Ciss with hate in her eyes.

'You two should get married quickly,' she said in an ugly voice. 'You are so much in love.'

Robert looked up at his mother. 'You believed that cousins should not marry, Mother,' he said quietly. 'You told me that often.'

'I do believe that cousins shouldn't marry,' replied Pauline. 'But you're not cousins. Your father was an Italian priest, Robert. He was a great man. And he was too great to have a weak son like you.'

With a terrible look on her face, Pauline left the room.

Pauline had gone mad. Her madness continued for a week. The doctor came and told her that she must sleep. He gave her drugs to help her. But she did not take the medicine. She walked about her room, looking ugly and full of hate. She would not look at either Robert or Ciss.

At first, Ciss was frightened by what she had done. She realized that her trick had made her aunt mad. Ciss almost felt sorry for the terrible thing that she had done.

Then she thought, 'This woman is the real Pauline. We never saw her true character before.'

But Pauline was not going to live long. She stayed in her room, and did not see anyone. She had her mirrors taken away. She did not want to look at herself.

Robert and Ciss spent a lot of time together. But Ciss could not tell Robert what she had done. She was afraid.

'Do you think that your mother ever loved anybody?' Ciss asked him one evening.

'Mother only loved herself!' Robert said. 'And she loved power. She got her power by controlling other people's lives. She was beautiful, and she grew strong by controlling everyone and everything. She destroyed Henry and she was destroying me.'

'And don't you forgive her?' asked Ciss.

'No, I don't. She took other people's hopes and happiness and destroyed them.'

Two days later, Pauline died.

Ciss found her dead, in her bed. Pauline's heart had become weak, and the drugs that she took were too strong for her. But after her death, Pauline got her revenge[55] on her son and her niece.

Pauline Attenborough was a very rich woman, but she left Robert only one thousand pounds. And she left Ciss only one hundred pounds. The rest of her money went to a museum. She had built a museum and given it her own name – the Pauline Attenborough Museum.

THE ROCKING HORSE[56] WINNER

Hester was a beautiful woman whose family was important and powerful. But she had no luck. Hester fell in love and got married. But her marriage became dull and empty. She had three beautiful children – a boy and two girls. But she did not love them. Hester pretended that she loved them, but she knew that she did not. Hester's husband travelled to the city each day and worked in an office. But he was not very successful in his job and did not earn much money. Hester did not know how to make money either. They both spent more money than they could earn. So they had serious money problems. Hester and her family lived in a fine house which had a pleasant garden. Beautiful and expensive things filled the house. The children had all the toys[57] that they wanted. But sometimes it seemed that a voice was whispering in the house. The children could hear the voice all the time. Nobody spoke about it, but the whisper was everywhere.

There must be more money! There must be more money!

Hester's son was called Paul.

'Mother,' said Paul, 'why don't we have our own car?'

'Because we're the poor members of the family,' she said.

'But why *are* we poor, Mother?' asked Paul.

When Hester replied, her voice was cold, hard and angry.

'Well,' she said slowly, 'it's because your father had no luck.'

'Is luck the same thing as money, Mother?'

'No, Paul. Luck brings money. If you're lucky, you have money. That's why it's better to be born lucky than rich. If you're rich, you may lose your money. But if you're lucky, you will always get more money.'

'Oh!' said Paul. 'And is Father not lucky?'

'He's very unlucky, I think,' said the mother bitterly.

'Well,' said Paul, '*I'm* a lucky person.'

'Excellent!' said Hester, laughing.

Paul saw that his mother did not believe him, and this made him angry. So the boy decided to try and find luck.

Paul had a rocking horse in the nursery, the room where the children played. While his sisters played with their dolls, Paul sat on the big wooden rocking horse and rode it madly. Then he stood in front of it, staring into its face. Its red mouth was slightly open, and its big glass eyes were wide and bright. 'Take me to the place where there is luck!' he said to the horse.

The horse could help him to find luck. That is what Paul believed. Sometimes he hit the horse on the neck, to make it go faster. He rode it more and more wildly, hoping for luck.

Paul's mother had a brother, Oscar Cresswell. One day Paul's mother and Uncle Oscar came to the nursery when Paul was riding his horse.

'Hello, young jockey[58]!' said Uncle Oscar. 'Is your horse going to win its race?'

Paul finished his mad ride and got down from the horse.

'What's the horse's name?' asked Uncle Oscar.

'He doesn't have just one name,' said Paul quietly. 'He has different names. He was called Sansovino last week.'

'Sansovino?' said Oscar. He was surprised. 'But that's the name of the horse which won the big race at Ascot[59]. How did you know that name?'

'He talks about horse-races with Bassett,' said Paul's sister.

Bassett was the young gardener who worked for Paul's parents. He had been Oscar Cresswell's servant in the war, when Oscar was an army officer. Bassett now worked in the garden of Paul's house. Bassett knew a lot about horse-racing. Oscar was very pleased that Paul was becoming interested in horse-racing too. He went to see Bassett to ask him a few questions about his nephew.

'Master Paul asks me a lot of questions about the races, sir,' said Bassett.

'And does he ever make a bet[60]?' asked Oscar.

'I don't want to tell you Master Paul's secrets,' said Bassett. 'Please will you ask him that question yourself?'

Oscar took Paul for a ride in his car. 'Tell me, Paul, do you ever bet money on a horse?' he asked.

'Do you think that I shouldn't?' asked Paul.

'No,' said his uncle. 'I hoped that you could give me a tip[61] for the next big race at Lincoln. What's your advice? Which horse is going to win?'

'It's going to be Daffodil,' said Paul.

Daffodil had not run in many races and had not been successful. No one expected Daffodil to win the race.

'Daffodil?' asked Oscar. 'Are you sure? What about Mirza?'

'I only know the winner,' said Paul. 'That's Daffodil. You won't give the information to anybody else, will you, Uncle? I promised Bassett that I wouldn't tell anyone. Bassett and I are partners. We share our information with each other.

'Bassett lent me five shillings to bet on my first racehorse,' Paul went on. 'But the horse lost. Then you gave me ten shillings. I bet that money on a horse, and it won! So I thought that you were lucky. But you won't tell anyone else, will you?'

'All right,' said Oscar. 'I'll keep your tip about Daffodil a secret. How much money are you going to bet on Daffodil?'

'Three hundred pounds,' said the boy in a serious voice.

Oscar was very surprised. Three hundred pounds was a huge amount of money. He laughed.

'Where is your three hundred pounds?' he asked.

'Bassett keeps it safely for me,' the boy replied.

'And how much is Bassett betting on Daffodil?'

'Perhaps a hundred and fifty pounds,' said Paul.

Oscar was silent. He was very surprised but he was also very interested. He decided to take Paul to the racecourse where Daffodil was racing. It was Paul's first visit to a race-meeting and his blue eyes shone with excitement. Daffodil won his race.

'I have one thousand, five hundred pounds now,' said Paul. 'Uncle, if you want to be a partner with Bassett and me, we could all be partners. But you must make a promise. You must never give the information about the winning horses to anybody else.'

The next afternoon, Oscar took Bassett and Paul to a park and they talked.

'If I'm sure about the winner, we're successful,' said Paul. 'But sometimes I'm not sure. Then we lose.'

'But when *are* you sure?' asked Uncle Oscar.

'It's Master Paul, sir,' said Bassett slowly, in a soft, quiet voice. 'Perhaps Heaven tells him. He was absolutely certain that Daffodil would win.'

'But where's the money that Paul has won?' asked Oscar.

'I keep it safely for him,' said Bassett. 'Whenever Master Paul wants the money, he can have it.'

'Fifteen hundred pounds!' said Oscar, shaking his head. He almost did not believe it.

'Yes,' said Bassett.

They drove home again. Oscar asked to see Paul's fifteen hundred pounds, and Bassett showed it to him. Then Oscar decided to become a partner too.

'Sometimes I'm absolutely sure which horse will win,' said Paul. 'I was sure about Daffodil. Sometimes I have an idea, and sometimes I have no idea at all, do I, Bassett? Then we have to be careful, because we lose.'

'And when you're sure, what makes you sure?' asked Oscar.

Paul looked uncomfortable. 'Oh, well, I don't know,' he said. 'I'm sure, Uncle. That's all.'

The next race was the Leger. Paul was 'sure' about the winner of this race. He bet a thousand pounds on a horse called Lively Spark. Lively Spark came in first place and

Paul won ten thousand pounds. Oscar Cresswell won two thousand pounds.

'You see,' said Paul. 'I was absolutely sure that Lively Spark would win.'

'I don't understand how you're guessing correctly,' said Oscar. 'What are you going to do with your money?'

'I wanted to get money for mother,' replied Paul. 'She said that she had no luck because father is unlucky. I want to be lucky. Then I can stop the whispers in our house.'

'Whispers in the house?' repeated Oscar in surprise. 'What do you mean?'

'Oh – oh, I don't know,' said Paul. 'But the house never has enough money. And so it's always whispering. I want to stop the whispers. But I don't want mother to know about my luck. She wouldn't let me bet on the horses.'

'Very well, Paul! We won't tell her,' said Oscar.

Paul and his uncle made a plan. Paul gave five thousand pounds to Oscar, and Oscar gave the money to a lawyer. The lawyer was going to tell Hester about a relative who she had never met. Hester was going to get five thousand pounds because the relative had died. Each year, on her birthday, Hester was going to receive one thousand pounds.

'So my sister will have a birthday present of a thousand pounds for the next five years!' said Oscar.

Paul's mother had her birthday in November. By that time, the whispers in the house had become very loud. Paul was worried.

Hester opened her letters at breakfast on her birthday.

Paul watched his mother's face carefully as she read the lawyer's letter. But she did not smile, her face became hard and cold.

'Did you have any presents for your birthday?' asked Paul.

'Not really,' said his mother. Then she went to the city.

In the afternoon, Oscar came to the house. He told Paul that his mother had been to see the lawyer. She had many large debts and she owed a lot of money to many people. So one thousand pounds was not enough for her. She wanted to have the whole amount. She wanted the five thousand pounds immediately.

'Oh, let her have all the money now,' said Paul. 'We can win some more money. We'll get a lot of money if I choose the winners of the Grand National, or the Lincolnshire, or the Derby. I'm sure to know the winner for *one* of these races.'

So Hester got the whole five thousand pounds. She spent a lot of money on new furniture and expensive things for the house. She told Paul that he would go to an expensive school in the autumn.

Then something very strange happened. The voices in the house suddenly changed. Before, they had only whispered. But now, they began to shout: *There must be more money! There must be more money!*

Paul was frightened. He spent a lot of time with Bassett. The day of the Grand National race arrived, but Paul was not sure about the name of the winner. He bet on the wrong horse and lost a hundred pounds. He did not know the winner for the Lincoln either, and he lost fifty pounds. He became very worried and his eyes were wild and strange.

'Don't worry about it, my boy!' said Oscar.

The next big race was the Derby.

'I *must* know the winner for the Derby!' said Paul. His big blue eyes shone strangely. Even his mother noticed that Paul did not look well.

'Perhaps you need a holiday,' she said. 'Would you like to go to the seaside? You'll feel better near the sea. The sun and fresh air will help you.'

'Mother, I can't go away before the Derby,' said Paul.

'You care too much about these horse-races,' Hester said. 'It's not good for you.'

'Please don't send me away until after the Derby,' said Paul. 'Don't send me away from this house.'

'Do you love this house so much?' asked his mother in surprise. 'I didn't know that. Very well. You can stay here until after the Derby.'

There was a secret reason why Paul wanted to stay in the house. He had not told anyone about it – not even Uncle Oscar or Bassett. His secret was his wooden rocking horse, which did not have a name. He asked for the horse to be moved to his bedroom.

'But aren't you too big for a rocking horse?' asked Hester.

'Well, I can't have a real horse of my own,' Paul said. 'And the rocking horse is a good friend to me.'

The time for the Derby was getting near. Paul behaved more and more strangely. He became very thin and his eyes were wild. His mother was worried about him.

Two nights before the Derby, Paul's mother and father were at a big party. Suddenly his mother felt worried about Paul. She telephoned the house and spoke to the children's governess[62].

'Is Master Paul all right?' asked Hester.

'Oh, yes,' said the governess in surprise. 'He's fine.'

Paul's parents got home at about one o'clock. The house was very quiet. Hester went upstairs to her son's room. She stood outside Paul's bedroom door, listening. A strange noise was coming from inside the room. Hester's heart gave a jump and almost stopped. What was that noise? The strange, mad sound went on and on. Hester had heard the sound before, but she did not know what it was.

Feeling very afraid, Hester slowly and carefully turned the handle of the door. The bedroom was dark. But near the window, she saw something moving wildly.

She switched on the light and stared in fear and surprise. Her son was wearing his pyjamas and riding on the wooden horse.

'Paul!' she cried. 'What are you doing?'

'It's Malabar!' the boy screamed in a loud, strange voice.

She switched on the light and stared in fear and surprise.

'It's Malabar!' He stared at his mother, his eyes shining with a strange fire. Then he stopped the horse and fell down onto the floor.

Hester ran to Paul, picked him up, and took him to his bed. His body was hot and he was very weak. He talked all the time in a wild, mad way. 'Malabar! It's Malabar!' he shouted. 'Bassett! Bassett, I *know*! It's Malabar!'

'Who or what is Malabar?' Hester asked her brother later. 'What does he mean?' Her heart felt as dead as a stone.

'It's the name of a racehorse,' said Oscar. 'Malabar is running in the Derby.'

Paul was very ill. But Oscar bet a thousand pounds on Malabar. On the third day of Paul's illness, his mother sat by his bed. Paul was not asleep, and he was not awake. His eyes stared ahead but saw nothing. They were like blue stones. His mother's heart felt like a stone too.

On the day of the Derby, Bassett came into the house in the evening. He wanted to see Paul. Paul's parents agreed and Bassett went into the boy's bedroom.

'Master Paul!' he whispered. 'Malabar came in first! It won! I did what you told me to do. I bet on Malabar. You now have eighty thousand pounds.'

Paul was very excited. He kept saying the same thing again and again. 'Malabar! Malabar! Do you think I'm lucky, Mother? I knew Malabar, didn't I? Eighty thousand pounds! That's lucky, isn't it, Mother? If I can ride my rocking horse, then I can be sure of the winner! Mother, did I ever tell you? I *am* lucky!'

'No, you never told me,' said his mother.

Later in the night, Paul died.

'My God,' said Oscar Cresswell to his sister. 'You've got eighty thousand pounds, but you've lost your son. Perhaps it's good that he's dead. Now Paul is at peace. He'll never have to ride a rocking horse again to find a winner.'

LOVE AMONG THE HAYSTACKS[63]

On the Wookeys' family farm, it was the time of the hay harvest[64]. During the harvest the dry grass, which had grown high all summer, was cut and cleared from the fields. Then the hay was piled up into huge haystacks. It was used to feed the farm animals during the winter.

There were two large fields on the farm. They were on the side of a hill which faced south. At the bottom of the hillside, there was a valley. The fields were divided by a hedge[65] that grew across the middle of both of them. In one of the fields, on the higher ground above the hedge, stood two huge haystacks. The hay was collected by farm workers. They put it into big wagons[66] that were pulled by large strong horses. When a wagon had been loaded[67] with hay, the wagon-driver drove it to the haystacks.

One of the stacks was now completed. It was tall and square and its top was covered by a stack-cloth – a big sheet of canvas[68]. Two brothers, Geoffrey and Maurice Wookey, were building the second haystack. They were standing on the top of the stack, waiting for a wagon to arrive with more hay. It was very hard work. The men had to lift the hay off the wagons with large forks and pile it onto the stack. Both brothers were hot and tired.

Maurice, the younger brother, was a handsome young man of twenty-one. His bright grey eyes were full of life and showed his strong feelings. He was careless and confident. He was happy with his life and never worried when things went wrong. Maurice knew what he wanted and did not care if people disagreed with him. Geoffrey was a year older than Maurice. His body was large and heavy, and he did not have the same self-confidence as Maurice.

Something had happened the night before, and now Maurice was laughing at Geoffrey.

The hay was harvested during two weeks of July. And each night during the harvest, one of the brothers slept in a shed beside the haystacks. They had to guard the tools. And if there was a storm, they had to cover the hay with a canvas stack-cloth.

Last night, Geoffrey had gone home because Maurice was going to watch the haystacks. Now Geoffrey was angry and jealous[69] of his brother. He had heard that a girl had visited Maurice in the evening.

Maurice threw himself down onto his back in the hay. He put his arms across his face and laughed. Geoffrey, who was standing over him, could see only his brother's red mouth. Maurice showed his teeth in a smile. He was making his brother feel jealous and he was enjoying it.

Geoffrey leaned on his hayfork, and looked across the valley to the land on the other side. He could see the town of Nottingham in the distance. The buildings of the town looked blue in the hot summer air. Geoffrey watched the wagon, loaded with hay, moving slowly up the hill towards them. As the big brown horse pulled the wagon up the hill, the wagon rocked like a ship on a golden yellow sea.

'You thought that I would be alone last night,' said Maurice, laughing excitedly. 'You didn't think that she would be with me.'

Geoffrey's face became red with anger and his blue eyes shone fiercely. He wanted to put his foot down on Maurice's mouth. The two brothers were both shy with girls. But the girl who had been with Maurice was different from all the other young women they had met. And she had not been born in England, she was a foreigner.

Beside the top field was the vicarage. The young foreign woman was working there. She was a governess. She taught the vicar's children their lessons. The girl's name was Paula

Jablonowsky. She was twenty years old and had golden blonde hair. She was slim and stepped lightly, like a cat. The vicar, a pale cold man, hated her.

One day, one of the vicar's children had run through a gap[70] in the hedge and into the field. The young woman had followed the child, calling out in German. When the young woman had fallen, Geoffrey had helped her to stand up.

At first, Paula had seemed to like Geoffrey. But later, she preferred[71] Maurice. Then last night, she had sat with Maurice as they looked at the moon. And she had let him kiss her.

Geoffrey looked towards the garden of the vicarage. He could see the girl there. She was wearing a golden-brown dress. He took off his hat, held up his right hand and waved a greeting to her. She waved too, but she did not seem very interested.

'She's waiting for Maurice,' Geoffrey thought. 'Why can't she love me, instead of him?

Maurice heard the voices of some men who were coming up the hill with a wagon. He stood up and saw the governess in the vicarage garden. He laughed and then waved to her. Geoffrey saw the young woman run from the garden, to a great tree in the field. As she looked at Maurice, she touched her lips with her fingers and kissed them again and again. Maurice laughed, took his red handkerchief from his neck, and waved the cloth towards her.

'Are you trying to warn us about something with that red handkerchief?' shouted a voice from below the stack. 'What's the danger?'

'Nothing,' said Maurice.

It was the brothers' father who was speaking. Mr Wookey had arrived with another load of hay. He saw the girl standing under the tree.

'Oh, so that's who is interesting you,' he said, looking at Maurice. He laughed.

Mr Wookey used his fork to pass the hay up to Geoffrey. Geoffrey then threw the hay across the stack, to Maurice. Maurice placed the hay around the top of the stack, building it higher and higher.

It was a very hot day. The sun was like a ball of fire in the pale sky. The three men did not speak to each other as they worked. Geoffrey was very angry with Maurice because of the foreign woman. He was not placing the hay where Maurice could pick it up easily. He was throwing it at his brother.

Geoffrey and his father were working together. They moved their forkfuls of hay faster and faster. But Maurice could not work as quickly. He did not have enough time to place the hay in the correct position on the stack. He began to get very angry. Sweat[72] was running down his face and into his eyes.

'That was the last wagon of hay,' said the father. He looked at the corner of the stack. 'There's something wrong with that corner,' he said. 'It's crooked[73]. It will make the stack weak. It might fall.'

Geoffrey, walked over to the corner of the stack and put his fork into the hay. He pushed down. The pile of hay shook.

'What are you doing, you fool!' shouted Maurice.

Geoffrey pushed his fork into the corner again. Maurice stepped across the top of the stack and pushed his brother. Geoffrey fell down onto the top of the haystack.

'Be careful who you push,' he said, as he stood up. 'And don't call me a fool again, do you hear?'

Maurice did not reply but started working around the top of the stack. Geoffrey stood on the top of the stack, looking out across the valley. He was as still as a statue[74].

'Are you going to move?' asked Maurice. He was holding a forkful of hay near his brother's feet. Geoffrey did not reply. Maurice tried to push him.

'Don't push me again!' said Geoffrey in a deep, dangerous voice.

'Move!' replied Maurice.

The brothers began to fight. They pushed against each other. But Geoffrey was heavier and stronger than Maurice. Maurice slipped and he fell over the edge of the high stack onto the hard ground.

Geoffrey's face became white with shock. He heard Maurice fall, but he could not move. Suddenly, he had no strength in his arms and legs. He was filled with fear.

'Father!' he shouted. 'Father!'

The men in the fields heard his shout and came running. The foreign governess ran towards the stack.

'Ah-h!' she cried out in a strange wild voice.

'What have you been doing?' Geoffrey heard his father ask. 'Maurice is dead! I shouldn't have put so much hay on the stack!'

There was a moment of silence. Then one of the workers said, 'He's not dead. He's moving.'

Geoffrey was glad that Maurice was not dead. But he hated himself now. He would never be as brave and careless as Maurice. And Maurice would tell everyone that Geoffrey had pushed him.

'He's opening his eyes!' shouted the girl, and she began to cry.

The vicar arrived. He had heard the shouts. Geoffrey heard him asking questions.

'What happened here?' the vicar said.

'His brother knocked him over,' said the governess.

'I don't think so,' said Mr Wookey to the vicar.

Maurice began to make soft sounds.

'What were you doing?' asked the father. 'Were you fighting with Geoffrey? Where is Geoffrey?'

Geoffrey climbed down the ladder which was beside the stack. He stood at the bottom and looked at his brother. Maurice was lying on some hay. His face was very pale. The young woman was kneeling[75] beside Maurice's head. The vicar was touching the young man's head, neck, chest, arms and legs. He wanted to find out if Maurice had any broken bones. Mr Wookey was kneeling on the other side of his son.

'I don't think that anything is broken,' said the vicar.

'*He* knocked him off the haystack,' said the girl, pointing at Geoffrey.

'No, he didn't,' said Maurice. 'I slipped and fell.'

'I think that you've made a mistake,' said Mr Wookey to the girl.

'Oh, no!' she cried. 'I saw him.' She lifted Maurice's head onto her lap[76]. Then she bent her head, until her face was close to Maurice's face.

'No, you're wrong,' said Maurice quietly. He did not want to say that Geoffrey had pushed him.

Maurice lay on the ground. His head was on the girl's lap. His face was pale, but he smiled as she leant over him.

When the girl looked up at Geoffrey, her pale blue eyes shone with anger.

'You want to get up?' the girl asked Maurice gently. She spoke English with a foreign accent[77].

'I'm in no hurry,' he replied. He was enjoying being close to the girl.

The vicar looked at the governess and the handsome young man.

'She's leaving us next month,' he said to Maurice's father. 'She's like a wild thing. She's disobedient and rude[78].'

Maurice laughed, showing his strong white teeth. The girl lifted his head from her lap and jumped up. She pulled Maurice to his feet before anyone could help. He was much taller than she. He put his hands on her shoulders, leant against her, and smiled.

'You all right?' she said happily.

'Yes, I am.'

He walked a few steps. 'There's nothing wrong with me, Father,' he said, laughing.

He put his hands on her shoulders, leant against her, and smiled.

'She's leaving at the end of three weeks,' said the vicar, coldly.

It was time for dinner. The food was brought into the fields on a small cart. The men stopped working. They were pleased to rest.

Maurice took a big basket that was covered with a cloth from the cart. In the basket, there was a huge meat pie, a dish of cold potatoes, some bread, and a large piece of cheese. There was tea to drink.

He walked to the tree near the stack and put the white cloth on the ground. The men took off their hats and wiped the sweat from their faces with large handkerchiefs. Then they sat on the ground under the great tree. While they ate their meal, they looked at the bright fields. The sun was high in the sky, the air was hot, and there was no wind. But it was cooler in the shade under the tree. The men ate and drank in silence. The father read a newspaper.

'She's here again!' called one of the men. The governess was coming across the field, carrying a plate.

'Are you bringing something for the sick man?' asked the father, laughing. 'He's feeling much better.'

'I am bringing him some chicken,' she said.

Maurice took the plate and ate the meat slowly. His face became red. He did not speak or look at the girl. He was shy. His father felt sorry for him.

'Come and sit by me,' Mr Wookey said to the girl. 'What's your name?'

The girl sat beside the father and looked at him with her pale blue eyes.

'My name is Paula Jablonowsky,' she said.

'What?' said Mr Wookey. 'Say your name again.'

The governess smiled and replied, 'Paula. My name is Paula.'

'Paula? No English women in this area have that name,'

said the man. He nodded towards his son. 'His name is —'

'I know it,' she said sweetly. 'His name is Maurice!' Then she looked into the father's eyes and laughed.

The men asked Paula questions about her family and her country. She told them that her father had been a shopkeeper in the German city of Hanover. But she had run away from her home because she did not like her father. Later, she had worked in a school for young ladies.

'What will you do when you leave the vicarage?'

'I will go to London, or to Paris. Or I'll get married,' she replied. The father laughed.

'Get married, eh? And who will you marry?'

'I don't know. I am going away.'

'Is the country too quiet for you?' asked the father. 'Wouldn't you like to marry a farmer? Then you could live on a farm and make butter and cheese.'

'Make butter?' She turned towards Maurice quickly, like a cat. Her eyes shone happily. 'I would like that.'

Suddenly a stranger came through the gap in the hedge and walked towards the tree. His body was small and thin, like the body of a wild animal. He had a short beard on his pointed chin. His clothes were old and torn, and the skin of his face and hands was red and dirty. He was a tramp[79].

'Have you any work for me?' the man asked.

'Any work?' said the father. 'We've almost finished our work here. Can't you see that? No, we've no work for you. You can have something to eat, if you like.'

The tramp was given the last piece of meat pie, which he ate greedily. The men watched him carefully.

'That was good,' he said.

'Do you want some bread and cheese?' asked the father.

'It will help to fill my stomach,' replied the tramp.

The man ate the bread and cheese more slowly. After the meal, all the men began to smoke their pipes[80].

'Can I have some tobacco?' asked the tramp.

The father gave him a little tobacco, and the tramp filled his own pipe. Then he smoked with the rest of the men. As they were sitting silently, another person came through the gap in the hedge. It was a young woman. She was small, and her hair was pulled tightly back under a hat.

'Have you got some work?' she asked the tramp.

'No, they haven't got any work for me.'

'Must I wait for you on the road all day?' she asked. 'Are you coming?'

'There's no reason to hurry,' said the tramp. 'If you wait, they might give *you* something to eat.'

'Have you had your dinner?' asked the father.

She looked at Mr Wookey angrily and turned away.

'Are you coming?' she asked the tramp again.

'He's had *his* dinner,' said the father. 'Do you want some?'

'He's finished our meat pie,' said Geoffrey, 'and a big piece of bread and cheese.'

'Well, it was given to me,' said the man.

Geoffrey and the young woman looked at each other. Suddenly Geoffrey seemed to know her feelings and she knew how he felt. They seemed to understand each other.

'There's a cake in the basket – you can have some of that,' said Maurice.

The woman turned and went away and the tramp stayed. Everyone looked at him angrily. They wanted him to leave.

'Aren't you going with your woman?' they said to the tramp.

The man stood up.

'Will you give me something for her?' he said. 'I don't *think* that she's had anything to eat today. But she gets more than I know about. I'm sure of that.'

Geoffrey passed him a piece of bread and some cheese, and the tramp pushed them into his pocket. He said nothing. Perhaps he was going to eat them later himself.

Geoffrey and Maurice worked hard all afternoon. The sun was extremely hot. The brothers had not spoken to each other since Maurice's fall. They were silent but they were friends now. Maurice was not going to say that Geoffrey had pushed him.

The work continued slowly. At five o'clock, all the men stopped and drank tea.

'We're not going to finish the harvest today,' said the father, as they sat under the tree.

'Then somebody will have to stay here tonight,' said Geoffrey. 'I'll stay.'

'No, I'll stay here,' said Maurice. He wanted to meet Paula.

At about eight o'clock, after the sun went down, the men got on their bicycles and rode away.

Paula was coming to meet Maurice at nine o'clock. He did not know what to do until she came. He decided to go and wash himself.

There was a cattle-trough[81] at one end of the hedge. Maurice washed his hands, arms and face in the cool water. It felt wonderful. Then he waited nervously by the tall hedge. Paula was late. She came at a quarter past nine.

'One of the children would not sleep,' she said.

Maurice laughed shyly. They walked away from the hedge and out across the field.

'I want to run!' she said suddenly.

'Let's run, then,' said Maurice.

She ran away quickly and he ran after her. Paula ran very fast, and it was difficult to catch her. Maurice put out his hand and caught her by the arm.

Three horses were standing in front of them in the field. Paula turned towards Maurice.

'Can we ride a horse?' she asked.

Maurice caught hold of the long mane[82] of a brown mare and led her to the stacks. In a shed near the haystacks, he found a halter[83]. He put it on the mare's head. The horse was big and strong. Maurice lifted Paula onto the mare's back, then climbed up in front of the girl. Then they rode up the hill together. When they reached the top of the hill, Maurice stopped the horse and they looked round.

The pale moon was shining in the night sky. On the left of the valley, Maurice and Paula could see a hill which was covered with dark trees. Down below them, small lights shone from the cottages in the valley. In the distance, they could see the lights of Nottingham. Paula put her arms around Maurice's waist. He wanted to turn and kiss her, but he was afraid.

The horse moved a few steps forward.

'Let her run!' cried Paula. 'Let her run fast!'

Maurice kicked his feet against the sides of the horse. The mare jumped forward and ran down the hill and across the field. Paula held Maurice tightly and leant her head on his back.

'We'll fall off! We'll fall off!' cried Maurice, laughing.

Paula pressed her body against him. At last the mare stopped. Paula got off the horse, and in a moment Maurice was standing beside her. They were both laughing and breathing quickly. Maurice held Paula in his arms and kissed her. Then, in silence, they walked towards the stacks.

Thick clouds had covered the moon and the sky was now quite dark. As they got near to the haystacks, Maurice felt a drop of rain on his face.

'There's going to be a storm,' he said. 'I'll have to get a stack-cloth and cover the top of the second stack. The cloths keep the rain off the stacks so that the hay doesn't get wet.'

He went to the shed and returned carrying a heavy cloth. Then he got a long ladder.

'Do you have to carry the cloth up there?' asked Paula, looking up at the top of the stack.

'Yes,' he answered.

He put the ladder against the side of the stack. He could not see the top.

A few drops of rain fell on the heavy cloth. It was very dark between the great stacks of hay. Paula looked up at the black wall of hay in front of her. She pressed her body against Maurice.

'Shall I help you?' she asked.

They opened the cloth on the ground. Then Maurice climbed up the tall ladder, pulling the stack-cloth behind him. Paula followed him up the ladder, carrying the other end of the cloth. They climbed up the ladder in silence.

As Maurice and Paula climbed up the stack, Geoffrey arrived on his bicycle. He had come to help Maurice put the cloth on the second stack. Geoffrey pushed his bicycle to the shed, but no one was there. He took the lamp from the front of his bicycle and walked round the stacks. Suddenly he saw a long ladder, which was against the stack, fall to the ground.

'What was that noise?' said a voice from the top of stack. It was his brother, Maurice.

Then Geoffrey heard a woman reply, 'Something fell.' It was the voice of the governess.

'It was the ladder,' said Maurice. He looked down from the top of the stack. 'We must have knocked it down with the cloth. Now we can't get down. But we can sit under the cloth. Then we won't get wet. But do you wish that you were safe in the vicarage? Should I shout for somebody? Do you want someone to come and help us?'

'No,' said the girl.

'Are you sure?' asked Maurice.

'Yes. I'm sure,' said the girl. She laughed.

Geoffrey turned away from the haystack. The rain was falling heavily now. He felt very lonely and sad as he went back to the shed. He was jealous of Maurice.

Geoffrey shone the lamp inside the shed. There were tools, things for horses and a deep pile of hay. Rain was falling heavily on the roof of the shed. Geoffrey lay on the hay, listened to the rain, and thought about Maurice and Paula. Geoffrey was in love with her. Why did Paula not love him? Why did she prefer Maurice?

Suddenly a black shadow came into the shed. Geoffrey's heart jumped in his chest. He was not afraid, but he was shocked. Someone was coming towards him. He stood up and held the person's arm.

'Who are you?' he said.

'Let me go!' said a woman's voice.

'What do you want?'

'I thought that *he* was here – the man you saw at dinner.'

It was the woman who had come looking for the tramp in the afternoon.

'Where did he leave you?' asked Geoffrey.

'I left him – here,' she replied. 'I've not seen him since dinner-time. He's my husband and he's not going to run away. I'll stop him.'

Geoffrey was silent. He did not know what to say.

'Are you wearing a coat ?' he asked at last. 'Are you cold?'

He lit a match. By its light, he saw that the woman's face was pale and she looked very tired. Rainwater was running from her old hat and her clothes were wet.

'You're very wet!' he said.

Geoffrey lit the bicycle lamp and the soft light shone in the little shed. There was a box in the corner of the building. Geoffrey took a blanket out of the box.

'Take off your hat and coat. I'll put this blanket around your shoulders,' he said.

The woman took off her coat. She was young – not much older than a girl. Geoffrey saw that her body was shaking.

'Is something wrong with you?' he asked. 'Are you ill?'

'I've been looking for my husband all day,' she said. 'I'm tired. I've walked a long way. And I haven't had anything to eat since morning.'

Geoffrey looked in the box again. There was some coffee, bread and cheese inside. The woman sat down on the bed of hay. Geoffrey took his knife and cut her a piece of bread and some cheese.

'I want some water,' she said.

Geoffrey picked up a can[84] and went out into the wet darkness. He walked down to the cattle-trough beside the great black hedge. Then he filled the can with water and returned to the shed. When he gave the can to the woman, her hands were shaking. She spilt some of the water from the can.

'Do you still feel bad?' he asked her. 'Can't you get warm?'

'Don't worry about me,' she replied. 'I'll go soon.'

'No, I don't want you to go,' said Geoffrey. 'I'm thinking about how you can get warm. I have to go and see if the stacks are safe. Take off your shoes and all your wet clothes. You can wrap yourself[85] in that blanket.'

Geoffrey went out and looked at the stacks. The cloths were still covering them. He could hear nothing but the sound of the rain falling on the canvas. Then he returned to the woman and sat beside her. The bicycle lamp was not lit now. They sat in the dark shed, listening to the sound of the rain.

'Is the man who came this afternoon truly your husband?' he asked.

'He is,' she answered.

'Do you follow him because you like him?'

'I don't like him – I wish that he was dead,' she said. 'But he's my husband. I married him when I was nineteen. We've been married for four years. He says that he's looking for a job. But he doesn't like work. He's lazy. We had a baby, but it died when it was ten months old. We've been travelling from town to town since my child died.'

'Are you warm now?' asked Geoffrey.

'I'm a little warmer – but my feet are very cold.'

'Let me warm them with my hands,' he said. The woman held out her feet and Geoffrey's large hands closed over them.

'They're as cold as ice!' he said.

Geoffrey rubbed her feet and tried to warm them. She leant forward and touched his hair gently.

'Do you feel better now?' he asked in a low voice.

Suddenly lifting his face towards her, he held out his hand to touch her hand. But in the darkness, he touched her face instead. It was wet with tears.

She pulled Geoffrey's head down and held his face against her breast. He put his arms round her and held her close. His body was warm and strong.

The woman put her arms around Geoffrey's neck. Then she turned her face and kissed his lips. It was his first romantic kiss.

When Geoffrey woke, the morning was cool and the sun was rising. The woman was lying in his arms, sleeping. Geoffrey held her very close. He did not feel lonely now. He felt confident, happy and complete.

The dawn came slowly. As the sky became lighter, Geoffrey could see that the rain had stopped falling. He looked down at the woman. She was watching him with her calm, golden-brown eyes. Immediately, she smiled. He smiled too and kissed her.

'What's your name?' he asked.

'Lydia,' she said.

'Lydia!' he repeated shyly. 'My name is Geoffrey Wookey.' They were silent for a few seconds.

'Will you go and look for your husband?' he asked.

'I'll have to,' she replied.

'Do you feel better now?' he asked in a low voice.

Geoffrey suddenly felt afraid. 'You mustn't,' he said. 'We could get married.'

'No.'

Geoffrey had thought many times about leaving the farm. He thought about living and working in another country – perhaps Canada. Now he had an idea. Perhaps he could ask this woman to go with him. Perhaps she would like the chance to leave her husband.

'Will you go to Canada with me?'

'Let's wait for two months. Your feelings might have changed by then,' she replied quietly.

'No,' said Geoffrey. 'My feelings will not have changed. I'll think the same things.' Then he said, 'Have you got any relatives? Can you stay with them?'

'I've got a sister who is married to a farm worker,' Lydia said. 'She lives in Crick. I can go and stay with her, if you want me to.'

Lydia agreed to go to her sister until spring. Then they would leave England by ship. They would sail to Canada. Geoffrey promised to write to Lydia at her sister's address.

A grey mist[86] was moving across the fields and hills. Geoffrey told her that his brother, Maurice, and Paula were on top of a stack. They could not get down from the haystack because the ladder had fallen.

'You should put the ladder against the stack again,' Lydia said. 'Go and do it now.'

Geoffrey walked to the stacks. The cold, grey mist moved between the tall piles of hay. There was no sound. Were Maurice and Paula up there? He lifted the ladder and put it against the side of the second stack. Suddenly, he heard Maurice's voice coming from the top of the stack.

'The ladder's here!' said his brother's voice.

'You said that it had fallen!' said Paula's voice.

'I heard it fall to the ground last night,' said Maurice. 'And I couldn't feel it or see it.'

'You lied to me,' said the German girl angrily. 'You made me stay here. You told me lies.'

'I told you the truth. The ladder had fallen.'

'Lies – lies – lies!' she cried. 'I'll never believe you again. You are bad – bad – bad.'

Now Maurice was angry too. 'Are you coming down?' he asked coldly.

'No, I don't want you.'

'Very well.'

Then Geoffrey saw his brother come down the ladder.

When Maurice reached the ground, he looked up. 'Are you coming?' he called again.

'No,' said Paula's voice. 'I won't come. You lied to me.'

For several minutes Maurice stood at the bottom of the ladder. He looked pale and cold.

'Are you coming?' he repeated. There was no reply.

'Then stay up there until you're ready,' he said and walked away. Around the other side of the stacks, he met Geoffrey.

'What are *you* doing here?' Maurice asked quickly.

'I've been here all night,' replied Geoffrey. 'I came to help you to cover the stack with the cloth. But I found that the cloth was already on the stack, and the ladder was down.'

'Did you put the ladder up again?'

'Yes – a few minutes ago. You remember the woman who was here yesterday, at dinner? She came back last night. She was looking for her husband. It was raining and she was wet. She stayed in the shed all night – with me. I'm going to give her some breakfast. It's the man who is bad, not her.'

'You do what you like,' said Maurice quietly. He seemed worried.

'What's the matter?' asked Geoffrey.

'Nothing,' said Maurice.

They went together to the shed. The woman was folding the blanket. She had washed her face and looked very pretty.

'I didn't think that I would find *you* here,' said Maurice. 'But it was better to be inside than outside last night.'

Geoffrey started to make a fire with some pieces of wood. Maurice went to find some more wood. Lydia got some coffee out of the box and Geoffrey started to boil some water in a can. They were preparing breakfast when Paula appeared. She had no hat and her face was very pale.

'Where is Maurice?' she asked Geoffrey.

'He's gone to get more wood. He'll be back soon.'

'When did you come?' Paula asked.

'I came last night,' said Geoffrey. 'I was going to put the cloth on the stack. But it was already covered. I couldn't see anyone near the stacks. I woke up half an hour ago, and put the ladder against the stack.'

Paula understood, and was silent. Now she knew that Maurice had not lied to her. The ladder *had* fallen and Geoffrey had put it up again. When Maurice returned a few minutes later, she was warming her hands at the fire. Maurice held his hands near the fire too.

'Are you cold?' Paula asked.

'A little,' Maurice answered.

They all sat round the fire, drinking the warm coffee and eating bread and cheese. Paula was sorry about what she had said to Maurice. She tried to make him look at her, but he would not. Geoffrey smiled at Lydia.

An hour later, Paula returned to the vicarage. Neither the vicar or his family knew that she had stayed all night on the haystack with Maurice.

By the end of the week, Paula was engaged to Maurice. When she had finished working at the vicarage, she went to live at the Wookeys' farm.

Geoffrey and Lydia kept their promise to each other. Lydia left her lazy husband and went to Canada with Geoffrey.

Points for Understanding

THE VIRGIN AND THE GIPSY

1 Why does the rector believe that Yvette will become like Cynthia?
2 Which superstition is talked about in this story?
3 Find the connections between the old gipsy woman's words and Yvette's life.

THE LOVELY LADY

1 Why do you think that Robert and Ciss are shy and dependent?
2 How does the relationship between Pauline, Robert and Ciss change after the summer storm? Why?

THE ROCKING HORSE WINNER

Why are these things important in the story?
(a) the voices in the house (b) Lively Spark (c) the winner of the Derby

LOVE AMONG THE HAYSTACKS

1 What are the Wookeys doing on the farm during two weeks in July?
2 Why is Geoffrey jealous of Maurice?
3 When do these people come to the haystacks and why?
(a) a young woman with a foreign accent, who steps lightly, like a cat
(b) a cold, pale man
(c) a small, thin man with a red and dirty face, who has old, torn clothes
(d) a man on a bicycle
(e) a woman with calm, golden-brown eyes

Glossary

1 ***county*** (page 4)
the United Kingdom of Great Britain is made up of England, Scotland, Wales and Northern Ireland. Each of these areas is divided into smaller areas called *counties*.

2 ***miner*** (page 4)
a man who digs deep under the ground for minerals such as coal, iron, gold, or silver.

3 ***quarrelled*** – *to quarrel* (page 4)
argue with someone who you know well.

4 ***sensitive*** (page 4)
a *sensitive* person sees and feels things quickly.

5 ***relationship*** (page 4)
the way that two or more things or people are connected with each other. If two people make love, they have a *sexual relationship* with each other.

6 ***won a scholarship*** (page 4)
sometimes very clever students from poor families can pass a special exam so that a school or college pays for their lessons, books, etc. In this way, students *win a scholarship* for their education.

7 ***got engaged*** – *to get engaged* (page 4)
when a man and a woman agree that they will marry, they *get engaged*. If a husband and wife no longer love each other and their marriage ends, they can *get a divorce*. After they have lived apart for several years, a judge agrees that the husband and wife can be divorced. At the beginning of the twentieth century, it was difficult for men and women to get divorced.

8 ***passionate*** (page 4)
a very strong feeling of love, hate, or anger is *passion*. A person who has these strong feelings is *passionate*.

9 ***the virgin and the gipsy*** (page 8)
a *virgin* is a young woman who has never had a sexual relationship with a man.
A *gipsy* is a member of a race of dark-haired, dark-eyed people called Romany. They speak Romany, their own language, and also the language of the country where they are living. The first Romanies might have come originally from Asia. Gipsies have their own beliefs and customs. Gipsies do not live in houses, they travel from place to place in caravans.
At the time of this story, gipsies' caravans were wooden vehicles which were pulled by horses.

Gipsies earned money by buying and selling horses. They made things like pots, pans and brushes, which they sold. And they were also fortune-tellers. They told people what would happen in their future lives.

10 ***vicar*** (page 8)
a Christian priest who is a member of the Church of England. *Vicars* work in churches. They live in *vicarages* with their families. A *rector* is more important than a vicar. He receives money from the people who pray in the church where he works. Rectors live in *rectories*.

11 ***neighbours*** (page 8)
people who live near you.

12 ***spoiled*** – *to spoil* (page 9)
change someone in a bad way, or harm them. A *spoiled* person gets everything that they want.

13 ***complain*** (page 9)
if you are unhappy about something and you speak about it, you are *complaining*. Your words are a *complaint*.

14 ***looking forward to*** – *to look forward to something* (page 9)
think happily about something that will happen in the future.

15 ***confident*** (page 10)
not feel nervous or frightened. If you believe that you are right and you are behaving correctly, you are *confident*. Someone behaves *confidently*, or has *self-confidence*, because they are not worried about anything.

16 ***depressed*** – *to be depressed* (page 10)
feel upset and unhappy about your life.

17 ***countryside*** (page 10)
the land outside towns, where there are farms, hills, etc., is called *countryside*. The word is often shortened to the *country*.

18 ***secretary*** (page 10)
a person who works in an office. A *secretary* writes letters and arranges meetings, etc.

19 ***picnic*** (page 11)
a meal which is eaten outside when the weather is fine.

20 ***not notice*** (page 12)
not see that there is anything wrong with a thing or a person.
If you see someone, and then think that they are interesting or attractive, you suddenly *notice* them. If you know that something or someone is near you, and you do nothing, you *take no notice of it/them*.

21 ***toad*** (page 13)
a small animal with brown skin, a wide mouth and a long tongue. *Toads* like to live in cool places. They eat insects and worms.

22 ***bee-hive*** (page 13)
bees are small insects with yellow and brown bodies. People keep bees in a large box called a *bee-hive*, when they want to get the sweet honey that the bees make.

23 ***winter camp*** (page 14)
a *camp* is a place where people live for a short time in tents, huts, or caravans. Between the months of November to March, the gipsies live in their *winter camp* near Bonsall Head.

24 ***wolf*** (page 15)
a wild animal that looks like a large dog.

25 ***nervously*** (page 15)
behave in a way that shows you are worried or afraid.

26 ***borrowed*** – *to borrow* (page 18)
use something that is owned by someone else. For example, if you *borrow* money from someone, you have to give all the money back to them in the future. The person who is giving this money is *lending* it to you.

27 ***felt guilty*** – *to feel guilty* (page 18)
guilt is the very strong feeling that you have when you know that you have done something wrong. When you have this uncomfortable feeling, you are *feeling guilty*.

28 ***trust yourself*** (page 18)
if you believe that someone is honest, kind and helpful, you *trust them*. If you believe that someone will say or do something which will hurt you, you *do not trust them*. You *distrust* that person. If you believe that your ideas and decisions are good, *you trust yourself*.

29 ***greedy*** (page 18)
greedy people have strong wishes for more things than they have. For example, they might want more money, food, or power.

30 ***spark*** (page 19)
a *spark* is a small flash of light or heat. Sparks can start a fire burning. A *spark of life* is a small sign that something is beginning to grow.

31 ***in a terrible mess*** (page 19)
the room has lots of things and pieces of cloth on the floor and the furniture. Also, some pieces of furniture are in the wrong place.

32 ***superstitious*** (page 20)
if you believe that special things bring good or bad luck, or are magic, you are *superstitious*.

Your thoughts about these signs of good or bad luck are your *superstitions*.

33 ***making a fuss*** – *to make a fuss* (page 20)
fuss is a worry about small things. If you speak of your worries about these things, you are *making a fuss*.

34 ***nerves*** (page 21)
nerves are your feelings. Granny is saying that Lucille becomes upset too easily and she must control these feelings.

35 ***desired*** – *to desire* (page 22)
want something very, very much.

36 ***pretended*** – *to pretend* (page 22)
do or say something that you do not really believe. Yvette has heard the gipsy, but she does not show that she has heard.

37 ***shadow*** (page 25)
a dark shape – an area of shade – which is made when a light shines behind something.

38 ***honeymoon*** (page 26)
after a man and woman get married, they have a holiday which is called a *honeymoon*.

39 ***engineer*** (page 26)
a person who designs bridges, roads, railways and machines, etc.

40 ***regiment*** (page 27)
a large group of soldiers who fight together. Soldiers *serve* – fight together – *in a regiment*.

41 ***renting*** – *to rent* (page 27)
when you pay to live in someone's house, you are *renting* that property. The money that you agree to pay every month, or every week, is the *rent*.

42 ***by accident*** (page 29)
if you were not expecting something to happen, it happens *by accident*. You can meet someone, or find something, by accident.

43 ***chimney*** (page 35)
a tall pipe in the wall of a house, which carries smoke from a fire up into the air. A *chimney* is usually made of stone or bricks.

44 ***towel*** (page 35)
a cloth which you use to dry your body when it is wet.

45 ***ladders*** (page 36)
you use a *ladder* to reach a high place. It is made of two long pieces of wood or metal that are joined by small pieces called rungs.

46 ***reservoir*** (page 37)
a place, like a lake, where water is kept. Water is brought from the *reservoir* to people's homes in pipes.

47 ***depended*** – *to depend on someone* (page 39)
need someone to help you, give you money, or a place to live. When someone gives you these things, you are *dependent* on that person. You are their *dependant*.
An *independent* person makes their own decisions about their life, their work, etc.

48 ***shy*** (page 39)
be nervous and worried when you meet someone.

49 ***chatted*** – *to chat* (page 40)
talk about pleasant and interesting things.

50 ***courtyard*** (page 40)
a space with buildings, or walls, around it.

51 ***flat*** (page 40)
a number of rooms where someone lives that are inside a larger house. Apartment is the American English word for a *flat*.

52 ***not my fault*** (page 41)
when you do something which makes a problem for another person, it *is your fault* that this has happened. If there is a problem and you did not make the trouble, you say: 'It *is not my fault*.'

53 ***sigh*** (page 42)
the soft sound that someone makes because they are sad, tired, or disappointed.

54 ***punish*** (page 46)
when someone does something wrong and you make them feel sorry, you are *punishing* them.

55 ***got her revenge*** (page 50)
Pauline has planned something bad for Robert and Ciss because they made her angry and upset.

56 ***rocking horse*** (page 51)
a wooden horse that is fastened to two long curved pieces of wood. The horse moves backwards and forwards when a child sits on it.

57 ***toys*** (page 51)
things which young children play with. For example, dolls and rocking horses are children's *toys*.

58 ***jockey*** (page 52)
a small, light person who rides racehorses.

59 ***Ascot*** (page 52)
the name of a place in southern England where horses run on a racecourse.
Names of famous horse races are 'the Derby', which takes place in Epsom – a town in southern England; and 'the Grand National', which takes place in Aintree – a town in northern England.

60 ***make a bet*** (page 53)
if you think that you know which horse will win a race, you pay money. This is called *making a bet*, or *putting money on* a horse. If the horse wins the race, you receive more money than you paid. This extra money is called your *winnings*.

61 ***give me a tip*** (page 53)
if you tell someone the name of a racehorse that will win a race, you are *giving* that person *a tip*.

62 ***governess*** (page 57)
a young, unmarried woman who lived in the house of a rich family and taught their children.

63 ***haystacks*** (page 60)
when grass has finished growing, it is cut and dried. The dried grass is called *hay* and it is fed to animals. When the hay is cut, it is kept together in a big pile called a *haystack*.

64 ***harvest*** (page 60)
when plants have finished growing and are ready to eat, they are *harvested*. The *harvest* is the time when these plants are taken from the ground.

65 ***hedge*** (page 60)
a line of trees or bushes that grow around the sides of a field is called a *hedge*. Hedges stop animals from leaving their fields.

66 ***wagons*** (page 60)
heavy wooden vehicles with four wheels which were pulled by strong horses.

67 ***loaded*** (page 60)
when something is very full, it is *loaded*. A *load* is a large amount of something that is carried by a person or a vehicle.

68 ***canvas*** (page 60)
strong cloth that water cannot get through.

69 ***jealous*** (page 61)
if someone has something that you want, or does something that you want to do, you are *jealous*. *Jealousy* is this feeling of sadness and anger.

70 ***gap*** (page 62)
a hole, or an opening, in a wall or a hedge (see Number 65).

71 ***preferred*** – *to prefer* (page 62)
like one person, or a thing, more than any another person, or thing.

72 ***sweat*** (page 63)
the water that comes out of your skin when you are hot, upset, or afraid.

73 ***crooked*** (page 63)
not straight. (Say: crook**ed**)

74 ***statue*** (page 63)
the figure of a person, or an animal, which is made in wood, stone, or metal.

75 ***kneeling*** – *to kneel* (page 64)
get down onto your knees on the ground.

76 ***lap*** (page 65)
the front part of a person's legs, from their knees to their waist.

77 ***foreign accent*** (page 65)
your *accent* is the way that you speak. You speak in the same way as the people where you grew up. Paula is a *foreigner*. She was born in Germany and is living in England. When she speaks English, she speaks the words with an accent of the place where she was born.

78 ***disobedient and rude*** (page 65)
a *rude* person says impolite and unkind things. A *disobedient* person never does what someone asks them to do.

79 ***tramp*** (page 68)
a person who moves from place to place and does not always work. *Tramps* often do not have homes of their own.

80 ***pipes*** (page 68)
thin tubes attached to small bowls which held tobacco. At this time, many men smoked tobacco in *pipes*. Cigarettes became more popular after the end of the First World War.

81 ***cattle-trough*** (page 70)
a container of water for cattle.

82 ***mane*** (page 70)
the long hair on the neck of a horse.

83 ***halter*** (page 71)
a strap that is put around the head of a horse so that you can lead the horse, or tie it to something. *Halters* are made of rope or leather.

84 ***can*** (page 74)
a small container made of metal.

85 ***wrap yourself*** (page 74)
Geoffrey is telling Lydia to put the blanket tightly around her body.

86 ***grey mist*** (page 77)
a thin cloud that comes close to the ground.

Exercises

Vocabulary: meanings of words from the story

Put the words and phrases in the box next to the correct meanings.

awful carelessly nervous evil blind apologize
spoiled complain caravan hay dishonest reservoir
adore engaged dull confident depressed countryside
rocking horse fortune secretary toad quarry fund
guilty liar thief selfish greedy sew

1		long grass that is cut, dried and used to feed animals
2		unable to see
3		(of a child or young person) behaves badly if not given what he or she wants
4		to say that you are not satisfied with something
5		to like someone or something very much
6		boring; (of weather) cloudy, not bright
7		believing in your own abilities and not feeling nervous or frightened
8		feeling unhappy because of a difficult or unpleasant situation
9		the area outside towns and cities, with farms, fields and trees
10		someone who works in an office and does jobs such as typing letters and answering phone calls
11		not thinking about what you are doing; not worrying about mistakes or accidents
12		a small animal that is similar to a frog; also an insulting word for an unpleasant person
13		luck; fate; what will happen to a person

14		a place where stone is dug out of the ground
15		a vehicle that you can live in
16		a formal collection of money for a particular purpose
17		ashamed and sorry because you have done something wrong
18		willing to tell lies, cheat and steal
19		a person who does not tell the truth
20		someone who steals something
21		thinking only about yourself and not caring about other people
22		wanting to eat and drink more food than you need
23		dreadful; terrible
24		to tell someone that you are sorry for doing something wrong or for causing a problem
25		very bad, cruel and wicked
26		related to anxious feelings that are difficult to control
27		to fasten something using a needle and thread
28		describing two people who have arranged to get married
29		a toy horse that a child can sit on and that moves forwards and backwards
30		an artificial lake where water is stored for supply to houses

Writing: rewrite sentences

Rewrite the sentences using the words and phrases in the box to replace the underlined words.

~~secretary~~ blind cart fortune spoiled caravan
selfish superstitious stool divorcing lucky awful
apologized sunbathe carelessly pale tramp whispers
guilty quarry complain depressed
countryside toad dishonest

Example: Lucille worked in an office.
You write: *Lucille worked as a secretary..*

1 The gipsy lived in a house on wheels.

---

2 Granny was old and couldn't see.

---

3 The gypsy told the girls what would happen to them in the future.

---

4 The rector let Yvette do what she wanted.

---

5 The gypsies camped by a place where stone is dug out of the ground.

---

6 Cissie had nothing to look forward to but she did not say she was unhappy.

---

7 Yvette ate all the little cakes without thinking of anyone else.

---

8 Life at the rectory made Yvette feel bored and unhappy.

---

9 The area around Papplewick was dark and dull.

---

10 Granny was an ugly, unpleasant old woman.

---

11 Aunt Cissie said that Yvette thought only about herself.

---

12 Granny believed in bad luck.

---

13 I'm talking about the people in this dreadful house.

---

14 Yvette had taken money which was not hers.

---

15 Stay in your room until you've said you're sorry.

---

16 He pulled a small chair from under a caravan.

---

17 My husband is legally ending our marriage.

---

18 They saw a horse pulling a small green vehicle with four wheels.

---

19 One afternoon, Ciss decided to lie in the sun too.

---

20 Aunt Pauline was feeling responsible for Henry's death.

---

21 Then I can stop the quiet voices in our house.

---

22 It's better to be born fortunate than rich.

---

23 His face was without colour.

---

24 He was a man who didn't have a home to go to.

Vocabulary: anagrams

The letters of each word are mixed up. Write the words correctly. The first one is an example.

Example: WROBOR

borrow — to take and use something for a short time then give it back

1	CTORYER	the house where a rector lives
2	SPWHREI	to talk very quietly
3	SOPAINS	a powerful emotion such as love or anger
4	CARVI	a priest in the Church of England
5	TTRGUE	a tube that collects rain water from the roof
6	SUVERNO	feeling excited or worried or slightly afraid
7	SIREED	to want something very much
8	DEPRENT	to behave in a way that makes others believe something that is not true
9	WASHDO	an area of darkness where something blocks the light
10	RNGSTAE	unusual or unexpected
11	MONEYHONO	a vacation that two people take after they are married
12	LARQUER	an argument, especially about some thing unimportant, between people who know each other well

13	TREN	an amount of money you pay regularly to use a house or room or office that belongs to someone else
14	CANTCIDE	something that happens unexpectedly such as a car crash
15	HYNMICE	a tube or passage that takes smoke away from a fire and out of a building
16	DRALED	a piece of equipment for reaching high places
17	NO DENDEP	rely on; also used when two or more things are connected and may vary
18	DRAYCROUT	a square area that is surrounded by buildings or walls
19	PSYIG	someone who moves around and doesn't live in one place for long
20	HUSPIN	to make someone suffer because they have done something wrong
21	VERGEEN	something that you do to hurt someone who has hurt you
22	KEYJOC	someone whose job is to ride horses in races
23	SHACKTAY	a large pile of dried grass on a farm
24	THARVES	the activity of collecting a crop
25	GHEDE	a line of bushes or small trees that grow closely together
26	NOWAG	a vehicle with four wheels that is used for carrying loads
27	SACVAN	strong, heavy cloth that is used for making tents and sails; it is also used by artists for painting pictures

28	ECCANT	a way of saying words that shows what country, region or social class someone comes from
29	HORGUT	a long narrow container that holds food or water for animals
30	TTGECOA	a small house usually in a village or the countryside

Grammar: syntax

Put the words into the correct order to make sentences.

Example: The stables of the afternoon sun shone hot on the flat roof.
You write: *The hot afternoon sun shone on the flat roof of the stables.*

1 Ciss turned of the ceiling switch suddenly on the light.

2 I marry that cousins shouldn't believe.

3 which I'm Sometimes sure will horse absolutely win.

4 What your do to you going with are money?

5 Paul was wanted a reason why to stay There in the secret house.

6 The pale ball of sky was like a sun in the fire.

7 The tramp woman stayed and turned away and the went.

8 Geoffrey and each Lydia kept other promise to their.

Vocabulary Choice: words which are related in meaning

Which word is most closely related? Look at the example and circle the word which is most closely related to the word in bold.

Example:
countryside national (area) passport native

1	**upset**	broken	spilled	upright	worried
2	**wagon**	horse	cart	load	station
3	**control**	manage	radio	contain	check
4	**selfish**	personal	private	greedy	generous
5	**modern**	present	old-fashioned	shy	traditional
6	**unclean**	bright	beautiful	ugly	dirty
7	**slippery**	icy	dry	comfortable	shoes
8	**caravan**	trailer	camel	donkey	trade
9	**honest**	lying	trustworthy	false	thief
10	**ghost**	hostess	writer	spirit	living
11	**wild**	tame	fierce	domestic	calm
12	**tip**	rubbish	suggestion	truck	bottom
13	**lend**	borrow	loan	curve	afford
14	**win**	succeed	lose	drop	spend
15	**partner**	rival	opponent	boss	associate

Macmillan Education
4 Crinan Street
London N1 9XW
A division of Macmillan Publishers Limited
Companies and representatives throughout the world

ISBN 978-0-230-03516-4
ISBN 978-1-4050-8735-3 (with CD edition)

These versions of the short stories, *The Virgin and the Gipsy*, *The Lovely Lady*, *The Rocking Horse Winner* and *Love Among the Haystacks* by D. H. Lawrence were retold by Anne Collins for Macmillan Readers
First published 2007

This version first published 2007

Illustrated by Julia Pearson
Cover by Getty Images/Hutton Archive

Printed and bound in Thailand

2014 2013 2012
6 5 4 3 2

with CD pack
2015 2014 2013
9 8 7 6 5